Jonathan Graf

The POWER of
PERSONAL PRAYER

Learning to Pray with Faith and Purpose

NAVPRESS

Bringing Truth to Life
P.O. Box 35001, Colorado Springs, Colorado 80935

OUR GUARANTEE TO YOU

We believe so strongly in the message of our books that we are making this quality guarantee to you. If for any reason you are disappointed with the content of this book, return the title page to us with your name and address and we will refund to you the list price of the book. To help us serve you better, please briefly describe why you were disappointed. Mail your refund request to: NavPress, P.O. Box 35002, Colorado Springs, CO 80935.

The Navigators is an international Christian organization. Our mission is to reach, disciple, and equip people to know Christ and to make Him known through successive generations. We envision multitudes of diverse people in the United States and every other nation who have a passionate love for Christ, live a lifestyle of sharing Christ's love, and multiply spiritual laborers among those without Christ.

NavPress is the publishing ministry of The Navigators. NavPress publications help believers learn biblical truth and apply what they learn to their lives and ministries. Our mission is to stimulate spiritual formation among our readers.

Library of Congress Catalog Card Number: 2001041042
ISBN 1-57683-275-9

Cover design by Jennifer Mahalik
Cover photo by Photodisc
Creative Team: Don Simpson, Greg Clouse, Amy Spencer, Glynese Northam

Some of the anecdotal illustrations in this book are true to life and are included with the permission of the persons involved. All other illustrations are composites of real situations, and any resemblance to people living or dead is coincidental.

Unless otherwise identified, all Scripture quotations in this publication are taken from the *HOLY BIBLE: NEW INTERNATIONAL VERSION®* (NIV®). Copyright © 1973, 1978, 1984 by International Bible Society. Used by permission of Zondervan Publishing House. All rights reserved. Other versions used include the *New King James Version* (NKJV), copyright © 1979, 1980, 1982, 1990, Thomas Nelson Inc., Publishers; and the *King James Version* (KJV).

Graf, Jonathan L.
  The power of personal prayer : learning to pray with faith and purpose / Jonathan Graf.
    p. cm.
  ISBN 1-57683-275-9 (pbk.)
  1. Prayer. I. Title.
  BV210.2 .G715 2002
  248.3'2--dc21   2001041042

FOR A FREE CATALOG OF
NAVPRESS BOOKS & BIBLE STUDIES,
CALL 1-800-366-7788 (USA)
OR 1-416-499-4615 (CANADA)

Printed in the United States of America

1 2 3 4 5 6 7 8 9 10 / 05 04 03 02 01

"Jon Graf has done a great service to everyone with a passion to pray with genuine faith and crystal clear purpose. Whether you are experiencing a new interest in prayer or have devoted yourself to intercession for many years, this book is filled with helpful insights. The Power of Personal Prayer examines and answers questions so many of us have been too rushed to ask, let alone to seek biblical answers. Jon's personal and biblical approach makes this a useful resource for every member of the prayer team, as well as ministry coordinators and those who teach others how to develop a life of prayer. If you carefully read and prayerfully apply Jon's teachings and insights, you will certainly (as he promises) 'Enjoy the ride!'"

—PHIL MIGLIORATTI, *National Pastors' Prayer Network*

"From years of leading everything from prayer retreats to city-wide prayer rallies, I have concluded: prayer is always better caught than taught. Yet, as Jon Graf knows (and says so effectively), there is still so much we can also learn about this extraordinary privilege. Having served with Jon in the national prayer movement the past ten years, I can assure you that no one is more in touch with its personal dimensions. His inspiring and insightful chapters will equip any Christian with fresh tools for a fulfilling personal prayer life. In this book, prayer is both taught and caught!"

—DAVID BRYANT, *chairman, America's National Prayer Committee; author, Messengers of Hope: Becoming Agents of Revival for the 21st Century*

"Jonathan Graf is devoted to prayer. However, he does not preach at the reader nor does he merely tell us that we ought to pray. Instead, he shares wonderful and practical insights on how to pray. This book will be a great help to all who read it."

—PAUL A. CEDAR, *D. Min.; chairman, Mission America*

—•— CONTENTS

—— FOREWORD

JON GRAF SHARES WONDERFUL NEWS IN *The Power of Personal Prayer:* You can learn to communicate with the only absolutely true, honest, caring being in the universe—God. Whether you are a shy new believer, an intimidated Christian who never has managed the knack of praying, or a mature intercessor, this book will guide you to the next fulfilling step in your prayer life.

It will teach you the simple basics and counteract theological errors that may be keeping your prayers ineffective. You will learn how you actually can talk to God and, if you listen, hear Him speak to you. It will show you how to grow an intimate relationship *with* God, not just know *about* Him. Then, as you understand and practice praying in His will, you will begin to actually help God run Planet Earth through your prayers. Surprisingly, you will become increasingly conscious of the things God did not do because nobody prayed.

How can all this happen? Jon advises: Just admit your struggles to God and sincerely and humbly step out in faith. Start small. Relax. The Holy Spirit is right inside you, ready to take your inadequate, even stumbling prayers to the Father according to God's will. Jon's teaching on disciplining yourself to have a definite, uninterrupted place to pray daily using various scriptural postures will help you experience exciting prayer times and help you grow in awesome intimacy with God.

Perhaps the most needed and least understood chapter is on *kingdom-focused prayer*. This is not just the praying for what we want—safety, healing, protection from persecution, a loved one not dying. No, it is learning to pray for God to answer with what He wants to do in and through that need. In my experience, very few people are praying on this level, yet I know it is the finest way to mature in prayer. It is exchanging our human wishes for the "so thats" of the God who never makes a mistake and knows the end He wants to accomplish with each trial and experience. Take time to thoroughly digest this chapter!

Using his own life's journey in prayer, not just theories, Jon gives this book wonderful authenticity. These teachings will increase the thrill and the power of your praying in proportion to the amount you actually pray.

The Power of Personal Prayer is full of little and big bites of prayer advice. Learn them one by one. Practice them. Then stand back in awe as you see the incredible prayer life you have longed for develop amazingly before your very eyes!

—*Evelyn Christenson*
St. Paul, Minnesota

—•— ACKNOWLEDGMENTS

WRITING A BOOK IS NEVER EASY ON ONE'S FAMILY, SO I WOULD like to thank my wife, JoLyn, and daughter, Amy, for their help. JoLyn didn't nag as I procrastinated, and both of them let me be when I got at it in earnest. And as only a spouse can do, JoLyn offered me helpful criticism on my more controversial material. I would also like to thank my parents, both for their dedication in praying for me over the years and for sharing the wonderful stories of answered prayer from their lives— many of which I never knew about until this year. Finally, I would like to thank Lee Brase, a mentor to me, for his helpful suggestions, and my editor, Greg Clouse, for his thoughtful and careful work on this book.

—•— INTRODUCTION

IT WAS SHORTLY AFTER MIDNIGHT ON WHAT HAD BEEN PROBABLY THE most draining day of my life. I was on the New York State Thruway making the fifth three-hour leg between Cato and Albany, New York.

Having loaded and unloaded my uncle's pickup truck twice, having sold a few earthly goods that wouldn't fit in the last trip, having emptied the house my wife and I had purchased only two years previous, I was beyond exhausted.

My wife of five years had left me, and I was moving to a new city, facing a new job, needing new friends. And feeling about as low as I have ever been.

It was there on the Thruway, trying to see through the blackness of the night and my tears, that I reached out to God in the most honest and sincere prayer I ever prayed, "God, help me. Help me to survive. Help me to see some hope."

It was also there that a most amazing thing happened. Within seconds a peace settled over me. My tears of pain suddenly turned to tears of thanks—and even joy. At the same time, a little chorus came on the Christian station I was listening to:

He will not let you fall,
He will not let you fall.
He is never weary,
He will not let you fall.

Over the next month I saw more answers to prayer than I have ever seen in my Christian walk—before or since. They were answers that showed me God would not let me fall. They were answers that settled for me, from that day forward, the truth that prayer works! Let me share two of the major ones.

Example number 1: I needed to purchase some furniture as I set up an apartment but had only $900 to spend on my living room. I found a sofa and love seat I really liked for $1,800, but I determined to buy a lesser-quality set in my price range. Just before I went back to the store to purchase the furniture, my aunt phoned. It was Labor Day weekend and she and my uncle were going to their cottage; did I want to come?

I forgot about the store and went, realizing that my set was only on sale that weekend. I prayed about it.

When I returned to the store Tuesday evening, sure enough the set had gone up to $1,200. Disappointed, I turned to go, only to notice a new sign on the set I had wanted all along. It read, "Close-out $900!"

Example number 2: Our house had been on the market for most of the summer with no bites, and a mortgage payment was soon coming due. Both my ex-wife and I had rents to pay, besides the mortgage. Where would the extra money come from? I tried prayer.

A few days later another aunt called me with an absolutely amazing "coincidence." She had run into an acquaintance from a former church, a woman I had dated seven years previous. This woman had gotten married in the meantime, and she and her husband had a leaky roof on their house. Knowing I had put myself through college doing roofing, she said to my aunt, "Too bad Jon's not around, we'd hire him to repair our roof." My aunt smiled and told her I had just moved to town.

Over the next two weekends I repaired their roof, and the roof on a rental property of her father's. I cleared—to the dollar—the amount I needed for the mortgage payment. Our house sold the next month.

Most of us can pray when we are in crisis, when we are desperate. But unfortunately, we often find it hard, awkward, even impossible to pray when times are good. As a result, many believers do not have regular, effective prayer lives.

Some would say this is because more than anything else Satan hates to see people pray. He hates to see churches pray. Why? Because prayer, along with Bible reading, is the most crucial element of our walk with Jesus Christ. We learn about God by reading the Bible—His Word; we experience God through prayer. It is our lifeline, our method of communicating with Him. And prayer moves the hand of God—it releases His will in our lives, and on earth.

But we can't give Satan all the credit for our anemic prayer lives. Much of our ineffectiveness, our inconsistency, is our own fault. We struggle in prayer for a variety of reasons. We were never really taught how to pray. Perhaps we prayed early in our relationship with God, but it seemed we hit a wall and saw fewer and fewer answers. Rather than figuring out what was wrong, we simply prayed less and less. Some of us had bad experiences. Well meaning, yet totally in error, friends told us we were doing something wrong. We weren't "claiming" our answer. Or we were too bold—after all, God is sovereign; you can't tell Him what to do. Perhaps the thing we desired and prayed fervently for never came to pass. So we quit praying, angry with God and disillusioned with prayer.

If you are a new believer, this book will help you understand some foundational keys to prayer and help you guard against those obstacles that creep in to rob believers of the lifeline of prayer. If you are a believer who wants to grow in your prayer life but are struggling in the process, this book will help you too. Prayer should be, and can be, an exciting, effective, and even fun part of your Christian walk.

And that is the goal of this book. By teaching the basics, by providing tips on how to pray more effectively, by offering some simple theology to counterbalance errors that you may have learned, I want to encourage and energize your passion for prayer.

Keep an open mind and an open heart, and continue reading. Your prayer life will never be the same.

Section 1

The FOUNDATIONS of
PRAYER

——1

WHAT IS PRAYER?

L ANI SAT IN THE DARK IN THE ROOM SHE AND HER HUSBAND HAD
prepared as a nursery for their new baby—only it was
not to be filled. Unable to sleep, trying to make sense of this
miscarriage following three years of infertility, she prayed. She
relates that there, for the first time, she heard the voice of God:
"I'm here. You're going to be all right."

I had recently married a single mom and was going
through the learning curve of having a daughter—an eight-
year-old—for the first time. It was late at night; Amy was in
pain with an earache. *Do I need to rush her to the emergency room?*
I wondered. I did what I knew to do. I laid hands on her ear and
asked God to heal her, to allow her to fall asleep. Within minutes she was resting peacefully, and soon was sound asleep.

Joyce heard the news of the escape of seven criminals from
a Texas prison. Even though the escape was more than a thousand miles away from her granddaughter, she felt compelled to
pray for her protection. She prayed for almost a month and
intensified her petitions when the shocking news came that five
of the criminals had been captured one town away from where
her granddaughter lived. A week later the two remaining fugi-
tives were captured just a few miles from her granddaughter's

17

house. Her prayers not only kept her granddaughter safe, but likely combined with the prayers of many others to weave a protective blanket over the area. Even though these men had murdered a police officer in Texas, they didn't harm anyone in Colorado Springs and gave up peacefully.

Carol, a mother of three, was driving on the expressway thirty miles from home. Suddenly she had a strong impression that she should pray for her children. Later she learned that at the very moment she was praying, her teenage son was in a classroom where the teacher was going on a godless tirade, spewing false ideas and philosophies.

A mystery! There's no other way to describe prayer. Think of it! If you have come into a relationship with Jesus Christ, you have the privilege of communicating with the Divine. You can talk to God. And, if you listen, you can hear Him speak too.

Simply put, prayer is communication with God. Some have defined it as "being with God."[1] I can talk to God any time of the day or night. Anywhere—whether in my favorite chair, walking the dog, driving the car, taking a shower, mowing the lawn, or sitting by a quiet stream in the mountains. Al Vander Griend calls prayer the "talking part of the most important love relationship in my life."[2]

Somehow, for some reason, almighty God has not only decided that He wants to be in relationship with us and communicate with us, but He also has provided the method to do it. Prayer. A. B. Simpson, founder of the Christian and Missionary Alliance, said it well a century ago: "The mystery of prayer! There is nothing like it in the natural universe . . . marvelous bond of prayer that can span the gulf between the Creator and the creature, the infinite God and the humblest and most illiterate child."[3]

While we cannot fully explain it, the fact remains: Prayer is an awesome privilege! If you are starting out on your faith journey, do everything you can to grow in prayer. It will bring adventure, mystery, and a sense of the presence of God into your life. Prayer will prove to be the key to a vibrant relationship with God.

As you start or grow your journey into prayer, you may be thinking, *Why should I pray? What are the reasons for prayer? Is it just to talk to God?*

—— REASONS FOR PRAYER

There are two main reasons for prayer.

1. Relationship. The primary purpose for prayer is to grow what Vander Griend calls "the most important love relationship in my life." God simply wants us to know Him. He wants to be in communion with us. He wants to talk to us, to have us share our hearts with Him.

When you are in a human relationship, it will not grow without regular communication. If you do not spend time with each other, talk to each other, share what's on your hearts and minds, then that relationship will go nowhere.

So it is with God. If we are to develop a relationship with Him, prayer becomes central. If we do not spend time with Him, if we do not talk to Him, if we do not listen to Him, we have no relationship. We can know *about* God by reading the Bible, but we cannot *know* God without prayer.

"You will seek me and find me," says God, "when you seek me with all your heart" (Jeremiah 29:13). To build this relationship we must take on the attitude of a seeker: I am not going to give up until I meet God. We need the attitude of the psalmist who said,

> As the deer pants for streams of water,
>   so my soul pants for you, O God.

My soul thirsts for God, for the living God.
When can I go and meet with God? . . .

By day the LORD directs his love,
at night his song is with me—
a prayer to the God of my life. (Psalm 42:1-2,8)

Jesus Himself should be our model. He both needed and desired time alone with God. Verse after verse tells us that He rose up early or spent all night talking with the Father. He received strength and counsel, direction and purpose from those times. They were so important to Him that Luke tells us that in the week leading up to His crucifixion, "Each day Jesus was teaching at the temple, and each evening he went out to spend the night on the hill called the Mount of Olives" (Luke 21:37). What did He do there? Spent time with God.

The apostle Paul declared, "I consider everything a loss compared to the surpassing greatness of knowing Christ Jesus my Lord" (Philippians 3:8). Paul probably didn't have the Gospels to get to know Jesus; he got to know Him through prayer.

How much more do we need to foster that relationship with God! Like King David, we need to say, "My heart says of you, 'Seek his face!' Your face, LORD, I will seek" (Psalm 27:8).

2. Releasing God's will. The second major purpose for prayer is that it releases God's will on earth. While I cannot explain how it works, somehow, in God's sovereign plan, He has chosen to accomplish certain aspects of His will only if people pray. Some believers cringe at this teaching. "What do you mean it releases God's will?" they say. "God's will is God's will. He's going to do it whether we pray or not." But Scripture, Christians of the past centuries, and experience all tell us otherwise.

What does Scripture say? Let's start with Elijah. James tells us, "Elijah was a man just like us. He prayed earnestly that it would not rain, and it did not rain on the land for three and a half years. Again he prayed, and the heavens gave rain, and the earth produced its crops" (James 5:17-18). First Kings 17 and 18 gives us the story of these two verses. God apparently put in Elijah's heart to pray that it wouldn't rain. The prophet went to King Ahab and declared it wouldn't rain for three years—and it didn't.

"After a long time, in the third year, the word of the LORD came to Elijah: 'Go and present yourself to Ahab, and I will send rain on the land'" (1 Kings 18:1). What follows is the incredible showdown between Elijah and the true God and the false prophets of Baal. Following a decisive victory, Elijah said to the king, "Go, eat and drink, for there is the sound of a heavy rain" (18:41). Then Scripture tells us,

> *Elijah climbed to the top of Carmel, bent down to the ground and put his face between his knees [signifying intense prayer].*
>
> *"Go and look toward the sea," he told his servant. And he went up and looked.*
>
> *"There is nothing there," he said.*
>
> *Seven times Elijah said, "Go back."*
>
> *The seventh time the servant reported, "A cloud as small as a man's hand is rising from the sea."*
>
> *So Elijah said, "Go and tell Ahab, 'Hitch up your chariot and go down before the rain stops you.'"*
>
> *Meanwhile, the sky grew black with clouds, the wind rose, [and] a heavy rain came on. (1 Kings 18:42-45)*

Did you notice the sequence? God planted a thought in Elijah—*pray for no rain*—then His will was released. He sent word again—*I'm going to send rain.* Yet somehow Elijah knew to pray fervently for it to happen. Again, God's will was released.

Daniel, a Hebrew exile in Babylon, had a similar experience. While reading Jeremiah's prophecies, Daniel discovered that Israel's captivity was to last seventy years and that the time was almost up. Shouldn't he have praised God and started anticipating this event? That's what I would have done. But Daniel "turned to the Lord God and pleaded with him in prayer and petition, in fasting, and in sackcloth and ashes" (Daniel 9:3). That's quite a reaction to something God said in Scripture was going to happen. Why would Daniel pray so? Maybe he just lacked faith to believe God's Word. I doubt that. I firmly believe that because of God's plan to include humans in the releasing of His will on earth, He drove Daniel to prayer.

Author Dutch Sheets, commenting on this experience, said, "No verse in Daniel specifically reports that Israel was restored because of Daniel's prayers, but the insinuation is there. We do know that an angel was dispatched immediately after Daniel started praying, for he tells Daniel, 'Your words were heard, and I have come in response to them' (Dan. 10:12)."[4]

We also have the chilling reverse proof—something doesn't happen because no one prays. According to Ezekiel 22, God was set to punish Israel for its sins, but would have shown mercy had someone righteous only prayed. Unfortunately, He found no such person:

"I looked for a man among them who would build up the wall and stand before me in the gap on behalf of the land so I would not have to destroy it, but I found none. So I will pour out my wrath on them and consume them with my fiery anger, bringing down on their own heads all they have done." (verses 30-31)

Clearly, Sheets comments, God was saying, "While My justice demanded judgment, My love wanted forgiveness. Had I been able to find a human to ask Me to spare this people, I could have done it. It would have allowed Me to show mercy. Because I found no one, however, I had to destroy them."[5]

Christian leaders of the past certainly taught this truth. John Wesley once said, "God does nothing on the earth save in answer to believing prayer." E. M. Bounds wrote,

> The prayers of God's saints are the capital stock in heaven by which Christ carries on His great work upon earth. The great throes and mighty convulsions on earth are the results of these prayers. Earth is changed, revolutionized; angels move on more powerful, more rapid wing, and God's policy is shaped as the prayers are more numerous, more efficient.[6]

Even modern experience bears out this truth. Today the medical community is starting to take notice of the power of prayer. Studies show that people who were prayed for, or who were praying people, fare far better in their healing journey than those for whom prayer was not involved. We all know people who seem to get their prayers answered more readily than others. We always ask them to pray for us. Why does this happen? Does God love them more? No. But He responds and His will is released because they take the time to pray, to ask.

Most of us have heard stories of individuals, who—like Joyce and Carol—are suddenly burdened to pray for some person or situation. Later they find out that something very serious was happening to the individual at that time. Why would God burden them to pray unless He needed them to pray to release His plan?

⸺ So Why Don't We Pray?

With all of these facts, one would think we believers would pray constantly, that we would thrive on prayer. Unfortunately, many Christians in Western culture do not avail themselves of the privilege of prayer. Why?

We know from Scripture that God values prayer. Jesus was constantly communicating with the Father through prayer, evidenced throughout the Gospel records in verses like, "Jesus often withdrew to lonely places and prayed" (Luke 5:16); or "Very early in the morning, while it was still dark, Jesus got up, left the house and went off to a solitary place, where he prayed" (Mark 1:35).

In fact, prayer is so important to God that He saves the prayers of the saints: "The twenty-four elders fell down before the Lamb. Each one had a harp and they were holding golden bowls full of incense, which are the prayers of the saints" (Revelation 5:8). A little later, as the last of the seven seals was opened, heaven fell silent for thirty minutes. During that time John observed, "Another angel, who had a golden censer, came and stood at the altar. He was given much incense to offer, with the prayers of all the saints, on the golden altar before the throne. The smoke of the incense, together with the prayers of the saints, went up before God from the angel's hand" (8:3-4). While I'm not sure what all that means, I am sure it indicates prayers are important to God.

The apostle Paul tells us, "The Spirit himself intercedes [prays] for us with groans that words cannot express. And he who searches our hearts knows the mind of the Spirit, because the Spirit intercedes for the saints in accordance with God's will" (Romans 8:26-27). And the writer of Hebrews reminds us that Jesus "always lives to intercede for [us]" (Hebrews 7:25).

Because God places so much emphasis on prayer, how

important it must be for us to practice it. So why don't we? If you are a new believer, coming to understand the following reasons will help guard against prayerlessness in your own life. If you are a struggler, find yourself here, and seek God's help.

── OBSTACLES TO PRAYER

1. Never learned how. The most common reason believers do not actively pray is that many of us never really learned how. Churches have the idea that prayer is so simple—and it is—that believers will just naturally learn it. But we don't. We don't pray because we fear we will "get it wrong." Yes, we know it is simply talking to God—and listening—but it intimidates us. Perhaps we listened to others pray long, flowery prayers and thought, *I can never pray like that!* Perhaps we did try, but somehow felt put down by others because of our simple attempts. Embarrassed, we stopped trying, shying away from situations where prayer played a role. We never went to a prayer meeting where we would be expected to pray out loud. We avoided small groups where prayer was a part. If we have a time of personal devotions, reading the Bible or a devotional book is all we do.

If you number yourself in that group, I have good news for you. You can learn to pray—this book will help. If your heart is sincere, it is virtually impossible to "get it wrong." You don't have to pray long, flowery prayers. They're fine for some people, but you can find your own prayer style. We all pray differently. Certain sects of monks practiced what some have called "breath prayer," which was simply uttering two- or three-word prayers ("Lord, I am a sinner," "Jesus be near," and the like) throughout the day. Classic author A. W. Tozer reminds us of Peter: "When Peter was starting to sink under those waters of Galilee, he had no time to consult the margin of someone's Bible to find out how he should pray. He just prayed out of his heart and out of his desperation, 'Lord, save me!'"[7] Prayers can be short, yet powerful and meaningful. If you are open for an adventure, keep reading.

2. Lost faith. Sadly, sometimes we no longer pray because we have lost faith in God to answer. We came to believe that prayer doesn't really work—at least for us. Maybe we started out trying this prayer stuff, but after a time we fell out of practice. We stopped seeing God answer prayer around us. Or we no longer felt He was hearing our prayers.

If you see yourself in this group, I have good news for you too. Prayer *does* work. God's promises regarding prayer are true. You probably need to tweak your thinking or perhaps deal with something that has become a stronghold blocking your relationship with God (see chapter 15). There is hope! Keep reading and start praying again!

3. A view of fate. Another reason believers do not pray: we subconsciously believe more in fate than in God's sovereignty, that "God is going to do His will whether I pray or not." And because we do not believe our prayers make a difference in the world, we do not pray. Often we think we are very spiritual because we hold onto the phrase "Remember, God is sovereign!" He is! But, as we have seen, God in His sovereignty has chosen to use the prayers of humans to release aspects of His will on earth. A believer who does not understand this truth will often succumb to a fatalistic view and will not pray about much.

If we do pray from time to time, we may also fall into this category when we are quick to use the phrase "if it be Your will" in our prayers. Yes, we should want God's will to be done, and we should want to pray His will. But that phrase often becomes a cop out for a lack of faith, or it rests on the belief that God is going to do His will regardless. In both situations, we fatalistically add the phrase to feel good.

I have to admit, this is the toughest belief system to overcome. I know, because this was me. Oh, I never would have said I had a fatalistic view of God's sovereignty when it came to prayer. But my prayer life reflected that I did. I was even proud of my "faith." I would pray about something once—or maybe twice—and pridefully resign myself to whatever happened. *Look how I'm surrendering to God's will,* I would think. What poppycock! It was a lack of faith that God would even answer my prayers. Pure and simple. I spent the better part of fifteen years in that rut. As a result, I wasn't much of a pray-er. God has brought me—and still is bringing me—out of that false mindset, so perhaps I have something to say to you too.

4. Thwarted by Satan. The final reason most believers do not have significant prayer lives is simply because of Satan himself. In fact, one could easily attribute the previous three reasons to the work of Satan as well. The Devil knows the power of prayer. He will do everything he possibly can to see that believers do not pray.

He will tell us we are doing it wrong. That God's not listening. That our faith isn't strong enough. And if we have unconfessed sin in our lives that puts a block between us and God (see chapter 15), Satan will convince us that we are fine.

Satan knows that God acts as a result of prayer. So he wants to keep us from it.

"In the spiritual world," said A. B. Simpson, "prayer is the potency that shakes the foundations of the kingdoms of darkness, that moves the hearts of men, and that works out the will of God."[8] He also wrote, "Satan runs away from a saint upon his knees."[9]

While this is true, remember, we can overcome this. "Submit yourselves, then, to God. Resist the devil, and he will flee from you" (James 4:7). What's the best way to resist the Devil? Pray! Pray even when you do not feel like it.

So What?

As we have seen, prayer is an awesome privilege. It is important to God, so it should be important to us. We also have to constantly ask ourselves, "What aspects of God's will in my life are not being released because of my lack of prayer? What blessings am I not receiving because I don't pray regularly?"

If you are a new believer, take prayer seriously, let it develop in your life, don't give up when it seems tough, and you are in for the time of your life! Imagine, communicating with God!

If you are a believer who doesn't pray consistently but wants to change, make a fresh start. Ask God to put a hunger for Himself and prayer within you. Get back up on the bike and ride.

What's the first step? "Come near to God and he will come near to you" (James 4:8). "Call to me," God says, "and I will answer you and tell you great and unsearchable things you do not know" (Jeremiah 33:3). Simply seek God. Ask Him for a desire to pray. Call to Him as Jeremiah says. Then watch what happens.

Though I had made a commitment to Jesus Christ at an early age and tried to live for Him off and on over the years, by the time I was twenty-three I was far from God. I was living a double life, involved in church but also into drugs and partying. That summer, before I was to start graduate school, I took a job as a night watchman at a Christian camp. I needed to "get my head together." God was starting to draw me back, though I didn't fully know it yet.

God had moved me to take the job, thus getting me in the middle of nowhere, away from my buddies and drug sources. He put some likeable Christian coworkers in my life, people whose relationships with God I admired. Finally, He brought it all together. He made me hungry for Him and put a "calling out" in my heart.

I come from a holiness tradition that develops great repentance preachers. We had one of those preachers during senior-high week at this camp—Robin Dimaggio. I was used to sitting under those preachers, and if you were not right with God, boy, you squirmed and felt guilt until you made a beeline for the altar to rededicate your life to God. That evening Robin was great. It was like he was preaching right at me. The double life, dabbling in sin, all of it. But the interesting thing was, I felt no guilt. About halfway through the sermon, I began to notice this. That got me to thinking, *Have I sunk so low? Have I fallen so far away from God that the Holy Spirit has left me?* I thought very analytically about it—again, no feeling of guilt or remorse, just wonderment.

Somewhere in the midst of my pondering, the altar call had started. As I sat there, a thought came to me—God's voice: *Ask Me to make you desire repentance.* I went down front, knelt at the altar, and simply called out to God. While I wasn't acting out of a guilty conscience like so many times before, I was sincere. "God, please give me a desire to repent of my lifestyle. I know I should, but I don't want to. If you change my heart, I want to serve You." And God answered. What came was a more profound and sincere remorse for my sin then I had ever felt before—or since. God met the cry of my heart that night and drew me back to Him.

Why do I tell you that story? Because if you desire to develop a prayer life, God will meet that desire. You start by simply coming to Him and telling Him of your desire. Ask Him to fill that desire with Himself.

For Further Reading

A Love Affair with God, C. Welton Gaddy (Broadman & Holman)
Disciple's Prayer Life, T.W. Hunt and Catherine Walker (LifeWay Press)
Live a Praying Life, Jennifer Kennedy Dean (The Master's Touch Publishing Company)

— 2

How Do I Pray?

M Y FRIEND JOE SELDOM PRAYS OUT LOUD IN OUR PRAYER GROUP —
yet he comes faithfully. While others bounce in and out
with short prayers four or more times during the forty-five-
minute prayer time, if he prays at all, Joe will only pray once. I
have heard him pray publicly, in a church service, and he prayed
eloquently, thoughtfully. He had been asked ahead of time, so he
was able to mentally prepare. I don't know why Joe doesn't pray
more freely. Perhaps he is like many people who want to pray,
but are somehow intimidated. It takes a lot to get them to venture out comfortably and freely in prayer.

Most of us take pride in doing things correctly. But some of us
take it a step further. If we can't do something well from the start,
we won't try it or do it at all. If the thing we are attempting doesn't
come easily, we quickly give up. We don't like to struggle.

Many of us are like that when it comes to prayer. We feel we
don't do it well, or perhaps we never learned how, so we don't
pray. We are confused that we have to struggle to grow our
prayer lives, so we give up trying. We hear eloquent pray-ers in
church and think, *That will never be me.*

For me, prayer has always been a struggle. My mind wanders
when I attempt to pray; I can't think of "meaningful" things to

31

pray for; I am bugged that I use the same phrases each time I pray. I was embarrassed that as the editor of a magazine on prayer I seldom could pray more than a few minutes at a time. All of these factors usually make prayer more a chore than a delight. And because it seemed a chore, for many years I neglected doing it—unless I was in a crisis or had a real need. But thankfully, I have grown over the years; I have learned to pray despite the struggle, to pray even when it seems a chore.

One thing I have learned over the past five years is that there is little I can do wrong in regard to prayer. I should not let my struggle and my impressions that I might be praying poorly deter me from praying at all. If you are letting your struggle with prayer keep you from praying, here are some truths that should encourage you.

—— TALKING TO GOD

Remember that prayer is simply talking to God and listening for His response. You can talk to Him just as you would talk to someone sitting right next to you. You do not have to use ornate language to talk to Him. You do not even need to worry if your prayer makes sense. God knows the heart, He knows your thoughts; you do not need to explain everything clearly for Him to understand. Coming to God is the important thing. He says, "Call upon me and come and pray to me, and I will listen to you. You will seek me and find me when you seek me with all your heart" (Jeremiah 29:12-13).

Sincerity and honesty are the most important issues when coming before God. While teaching His disciples about prayer, Jesus used a parable that showcased two different pray-ers.

> *"Two men went up to the temple to pray, one a Pharisee and the other a tax collector. The Pharisee stood up and prayed*

about himself: 'God, I thank you that I am not like other men — robbers, evildoers, adulterers — or even like this tax collector. I fast twice a week and give a tenth of all I get.'

"But the tax collector stood at a distance. He would not even look up to heaven, but beat his breast and said, 'God, have mercy on me, a sinner.'

"I tell you that this man, rather than the other, went home justified before God. For everyone who exalts himself will be humbled, and he who humbles himself will be exalted." (Luke 18:10-14)

Earlier, in the Sermon on the Mount, Jesus had taught some other principles regarding how we should pray. He taught simplicity over ornateness:

"When you pray, do not be like the hypocrites, for they love to pray standing in the synagogues and on the street corners to be seen by men. . . . But when you pray, go into your room, close the door and pray to your Father, who is unseen. . . . When you pray, do not keep on babbling like pagans, for they think they will be heard because of their many words. Do not be like them, for your Father knows what you need before you ask him." (Matthew 6:5-8)

While these verses certainly focus on humility in prayer, they also speak to the language we use. God simply wants us to humbly come to Him and share our hearts. We do not need to worry about how we phrase something — in fact, when we do worry about such matters, pride is taking over. Remember, the simple prayer of the thief on the cross, "Jesus, remember me when you come into your kingdom" (Luke 23:42), was enough to change the man for all eternity!

— — DON'T FORGET TO LISTEN

Remember too that a major part of prayer is listening for God to speak. We need not stress out about filling time with words when we pray ("I want to pray for thirty minutes so I'd better have enough things to talk about"). Reserve space for listening. Perhaps God will speak as you meditate on a verse of Scripture or as you wrestle over what to do in a particular situation. Maybe a thought will come to you while pausing in your prayers, and you will feel peace settling over you. That's hearing God (more about that in chapter 7).

I pause often when I pray—to leave space for God to speak. Because my longest time of prayer is early in the morning, I have even started to drift off to sleep as I paused. At first I stressed out about that and chided myself for being so weak. But then I realized I shouldn't sweat it. Early Christian fathers described that as "spiritual drowsiness" and felt it was a good thing.

— — THE HOLY SPIRIT PRAYS FOR US

Another principle about prayer that frees us from struggling: We can't get it wrong, because the Holy Spirit prays what we should be praying for. "The Spirit helps us in our weakness. We do not know what we ought to pray for, but the Spirit himself intercedes for us with groans that words cannot express. And he who searches our hearts knows the mind of the Spirit, because the Spirit intercedes for the saints in accordance with God's will" (Romans 8:26-27).

I don't believe this verse teaches that we need never pray because the Holy Spirit is praying for us. Rather, I believe it means that the Holy Spirit takes our feeble attempts to pray, our bumbling words, our incoherent and wandering thoughts, and turns them into powerful prayer. We still need to pray to make the "formula" work.

— — PRAYERS CAN BE SHORT

If you are just starting out on the journey into prayer, don't be bothered by the length of your prayers. Remember what Jesus said about "babbling" (Matthew 6:7). A sincere, three-sentence prayer, "Father, Amy [my daughter] needs to see Jesus in her struggle with being picked on by her classmates. I hurt because she hurts, and I know You hurt too. Please show her Your love at this time. In Jesus' name, amen," can have as much or even more impact than twenty minutes of rambling.

SO WHAT?

To begin to grow in prayer, start by picking two or three areas of your life in which you want to see God's hand at work. Maybe it's your kids, your relationship with your spouse, a work situation, a character flaw. As you seek to develop your prayer life, simply focus on these things. Don't worry about how long you pray—just talk to God about what's on your heart.

Read some Scripture, looking for God to speak to you out of His Word. As you pray, pause to listen from time to time. If a thought on the issue enters your mind, pray about that thought. Ask God to give you a promise from His Word regarding your situation (see chapter 14). Then pray over that verse.

You will be surprised how your prayer time grows. Eventually, you will feel confident to add other prayer items to your list, including ones beyond family or personal issues. Perhaps you will begin praying significantly for your pastor or your church, or maybe a neighbor who needs to meet Jesus.

The point is, don't chide yourself on how little you pray. Just try to develop some consistency with the fact that you do pray. God will do the rest.

Getting comfortable will also help you pray. While I am a proponent of a morning "quiet time" (a set time each day to read Scripture and pray), I encourage struggling and beginning pray-ers to find what works for them. Don't force yourself into a pattern that might not fit who you are. Do you walk each day? Pray while you walk. Do you have a significant commute each day (fifteen minutes or more)? Pray while you drive. You do not have to sit in the same chair in your living room for prayer to be effective.

But my mind will wander if I pray when I walk or drive, you might be thinking. So what?! When you walk with a friend and are deep in conversation, plenty of things might interrupt your conversation—another person coming toward you, a squirrel darting across your path, a siren in the distance. You pick your conversation up again. The same can happen if you're praying. In a real sense, Jesus is walking with you. If something interrupts your conversation, simply start talking again.

This prayer stuff is not as difficult as we often make it out to be. Just talk about what's on your mind—and listen. No special words, no props needed. Just you and God.

For Further Reading

A Love Affair with God, C. Welton Gaddy (Broadman & Holman)
The Art of Prayer, Timothy Jones (Ballantine Books)

--3

WHERE DO 1 PRAY?

I REMEMBER AS A YOUNG BOY OFTEN SEEING MY PARENTS' BEDROOM door open a crack and my mother kneeling in prayer beside the bed. I somehow knew I wasn't to disturb her there because something intimate was taking place. I later learned that this was Mom's place to daily meet with God.

As I grew older, I think one of the reasons I always struggled with prayer was that I never found a special place to pray, a place many Christians dub their "prayer closet." In the Sermon on the Mount, Jesus matter-of-factly said, "When you pray, go into your room, close the door and pray" (Matthew 6:6). The King James Version says, "Enter into thy closet," which is where the term "prayer closet" comes from.

Does that verse mean we are to remove the shoes, clothes, and boxes from one of our closets and use that space for prayer? No, the verse is not a command. Jesus was simply saying, "Don't make a show of your prayers." Actually, the room Jesus was likely referring to was the storage room. Most Jewish houses of that day had two rooms—a large room for living and a storage room for food provisions. The storage room was the only room that may have had a door to keep critters out. But, while I cannot see a scriptural command to have a prayer closet, there is a profound benefit from having a specific location in which to pray.

My assistant, Sandie Higley, literally did clean out a three-by-six closet of shoes, clothes, and boxes, and made it her place of prayer. She wrote an article in *Pray!* magazine about the experience:

> I began to feel God's pleasure at having made Him a sole priority in this area of my home.
>
> I can — and do — pray anywhere. We are to pray without ceasing, which indicates an attitude of prayer throughout the day — no matter where we are. But real intimacy with God occurs when we come aside with Him to a quiet place. . . .
>
> I feel the same sense of business with God when I enter my prayer closet. The things that otherwise distract my focus and attention are shut out instantly when I close that door. No one disturbs me there. The Father has my undivided attention, and I have His.[1]

Jesus didn't have a "closet." But He did have a time and place to pray. Many Scriptures refer to His going away by Himself at night or early in the morning to pray. He probably found a quiet, secluded place to meet the Father. "Your 'closet,'" said Sandie, "doesn't literally have to be a closet. It just has to be a spot that belongs only to the two of you, a place that honors and delights the Father and gives Him the opportunity to honor and delight you in return."[2]

For me, a specific chair in my bedroom serves the purpose. I get a cup of coffee and my Bible, and meet God in that chair each day. My little dog, Oscar, loves to join me, curling up on my lap as I begin to read. He is so used to my routine that he often heads for the chair without me at that time of the day.

—— Is Location Important?

So, am I saying that you have to have a specific place in which to pray? No. But if you want to get to the maturity level where you make time for prayer every day, having a specific place helps. It provides discipline, and more importantly, it makes it easier to enter the Lord's presence. As Sandie indicated, the things that distract your focus are not present when you have a specific place.

The key is to find a setting where you will not be interrupted. That may mean setting up a literal prayer closet. If you have the space in which to do that, I highly recommend it. Prayer warrior Dick Eastman once put a storage shed in his basement (complete with carpeted floor and walls) to serve as his prayer closet. In his current house, he built a little room under the stairs to his basement. If you set up a specific closet, you can decorate it with things that will turn your heart toward prayer—prayer lists, Scripture, world maps, photos of those for whom you regularly pray, and so on.

For most of us this will mean finding the room in our house where we are least likely to be disturbed, or where we are most comfortable. However, for some, sitting in one spot may not be conducive to disciplined praying. For you, finding a place where you can move is important. Do you know that prayerwalking is a perfectly legitimate form of praying? Take a walk and commune with God as you go. It may even help you to focus better. Perhaps some of your neighbors are on your prayer list. Thoughts of what to pray will come far more easily if you walk by their house rather than sit in your bedroom.

Remember, you can pray anywhere, at any time. Having a regular place simply makes communing with God easier.

⸺ WHAT ABOUT POSITIONS?

If you are having trouble staying focused while you pray, there are other things you can do as well. Perhaps changing your position from time to time would help. Scripture and other cultures provide a number of prayer positions you might try. Each has special significance. Most of the following positions and their meanings come from the article "Body Language: Praying with Your Whole Self," by David Trembley.[3]

On your face. Praying flat on your face can suggest humility. Jesus did it in the garden on the night He was betrayed: "Going a little farther, he fell with his face to the ground and prayed" (Matthew 26:39). Lying prostrate can be an excellent position because it shows a recognition of who we are—sinners—and who God is—holy and above us. It may not be a good position if you continue to fall asleep!

On your knees. This used to be the position everyone took when in a church prayer meeting. Today it has fallen on hard times as we prefer to be more comfortable sitting in our chairs. But it too shows humility and respect. People bow before kings and we are coming into the presence of the King of kings when we pray.

With your hands lifted. Exodus 17 tells the story of the Israelites's battle with the Amalekites. When Moses lifted his hands, the tide shifted to the Israelites; when he dropped his arms, the Amalekites started winning. Praying with your hands raised can be a symbol of victory, of praise, or of wanting to receive.

On your back. Praying while lying flat on your back can suggest wonder and willingness. It is a position of receiving. Trembley suggests: "Try this experiment. Lie face down and attend to God's presence. Speak and listen until you believe that the time of prayer is finished. Then roll over on your back and begin to pray again. Experience what happens to your prayers when you change positions."[4]

Pacing. A number of cultures pace about the room when they pray. If you are an active person, this posture might be best because it allows for an intensity in your praying.

So What?

So what does it all mean? While there are no hard and fast rules about having a place to pray, the practice clearly has benefits. If you have never done so, I recommend seeking a specific location in which to have a time of Bible reading and prayer each day. Then pick a time. If you are a morning person, set your time early. If you are a night person who needs to relax and unwind, pick a time in the evening. Prayer will become easier as it becomes more regular.

If you have tried all that and prayer still has not become more regular in your life, try prayerwalking or experimenting with various positions.

I actually began to become disciplined in my prayer life by learning to pray in the car. In 1988 and 1989, my job was thirty miles from home. I used my forty-minute commute to pray. I would often pop a worship tape in the car's tape player as background and just meet the Lord. It really made my day. In my next job, my commute was shorter, but I still used the time to pray. On that commute I even used specific traffic lights to remind me to pray for specific things. One long light in particular used to remind me to pray for my pastor. If it was green as I approached, I would even slow down to give it time to change. An especially long light, this gave me more than three minutes to uphold my pastor each day.

The point is, experiment with location and place until you find a solution that moves you toward more regular and significant prayer.

For Further Reading

"So What's the Big Deal about a Prayer Closet?" Sandie Higley *(Pray!* Issue 7, July/August 1998). Go to *www.praymag.com*, click on "Search the Archives," and type in "closet" on the search mechanism.

"Body Language: Praying with Your Whole Self," David Trembley (*Pray!* Issue 12, May/June 1999). Click on "Search the Archives" at www.praymag.com and type in "body" on the search mechanism.

— 4

TO WHOM SHOULD I PRAY?

"HOLY SPIRIT, YOU ARE WELCOME IN THIS PLACE," MIKE CRIED out to God again and again. A prayer group of pastors and I were in a circle, holding hands as we sought God's blessing for the conference that was starting in a few minutes.

As we prayed, a sense of peace settled over us. It turned out to be one of the most powerful conferences at which I have ever spoken. God's presence was evident from the start, and each session saw responsive people make life-changing decisions. The Holy Spirit was indeed present in that place—which happened to be a bare, steel and concrete building at a California state park campground.

You don't have to be a Christian for long before you hear people praying to different persons of the Trinity. "O God" or "Father God," "Jesus, You have said in Your Word," "Holy Spirit, come upon us now," and similar phrases are common across denominational lines.

But perhaps the question lingers: *To whom should I pray? Is it possible to pray to the wrong Person of the Trinity and thus have my prayers go unanswered? Are there rules to follow?*

▬▬ GOOD NEWS!

Relax! You cannot get it wrong. Remember that Father, Son, and Holy Spirit are all the same—they are God. When you pray to the Holy Spirit, you are praying to God. When you pray to Jesus, you are praying to God. When you pray to the Father, you are praying to God.

Now while that is true, you may still be thinking, *Are there principles I need to follow? Does Scripture teach anything about this topic?*

In the Old Testament, God was the only Person of the Trinity known to the Israelites. In the Psalms, David mostly prayed, "O God." He also addressed Him as "LORD," but even then he obviously was still referring to God in the nontrinitarian sense.

In the New Testament, Jesus taught His disciples to pray, "Our *Father* in heaven, hallowed be your name" (Matthew 6:9, emphasis added). We refer to this passage as "the Lord's Prayer." It is Jesus' only direct teaching on prayer. On numerous other occasions, Jesus prayed to the Father. Again, there was no real background yet, no teaching on the other members of the Trinity. Most people did not yet understand Jesus to be God, and He hadn't taught yet on the Holy Spirit, the Comforter who was to come. And when Jesus was on earth, He wasn't going to pray to Himself! So we have no incidents of Jesus praying to anyone other than God the Father.

Because Jesus prayed to the Father, most often people address God or the Father when they pray. Many churches of various denominations teach that you ought to pray to the Father through the Son—or in other words, in Jesus' name. And that method is correct. But it is also appropriate to pray to Jesus and the Holy Spirit, and scriptural precedents exist for doing so.

━ ━ THE EARLY CHURCH

In the Gospels we see that a number of people call out to Jesus. Bartimaeus, a blind beggar, cried out to Jesus, "Jesus, Son of David, have mercy on me" (Mark 10:47), and he was healed. The thief on the cross asked Jesus to remember him in His kingdom, and Jesus responded, "Today you will be with me in paradise" (Luke 23:43). I'm not sure these can be proof texts to support praying to Jesus, but they show that people recognized His divine power and were starting to call out to it.

In Acts, we see indications that the disciples had started praying in Jesus' name. When Peter and John healed the crippled man at the temple, they explained it by saying, "By faith in the name of Jesus, this man whom you see and know was made strong. It is Jesus' name and the faith that comes through him that has given this complete healing to him, as you can all see" (Acts 3:16).

If we go back to the actual healing, Peter declared, "Silver or gold I do not have, but what I have I give you. In the name of Jesus Christ of Nazareth, walk" (3:6).

When he was being martyred, Stephen prayed, "'Lord Jesus, receive my spirit.' Then he fell on his knees and cried out, 'Lord, do not hold this sin against them.' When he had said this, he fell asleep" (7:59-60).

As you study Acts, you will see that more and more the Father, Jesus, and the Holy Spirit become almost interchangeable. And they should; they are all God.

In Saul's Damascus Road experience, it was Jesus who talked to him.

> *[Saul] fell to the ground and heard a voice say to him,*
> *"Saul, Saul, why do you persecute me?"*
> *"Who are you, Lord?" Saul asked.*

"I am Jesus, whom you are persecuting," he replied. "Now get up and go into the city, and you will be told what you must do." (Acts 9:4-6)

Hours later, when Jesus spoke to Ananias, telling him to go to Saul, he replied: "Lord, . . . I have heard many reports about this man and all the harm he has done to your saints in Jerusalem. And he has come here with authority from the chief priests to arrest all who *call on your name"* (9:13-14, emphasis added). Jewish leaders were not arresting those who called on God's name, only those who called on Jesus' name. Ananias clearly was speaking to Jesus here (but of course, he was speaking to God).

Throughout Acts, there seems to be no indication that Paul *wasn't* praying to Jesus as God. At one point, when testifying to a hostile crowd, he referred back to his Damascus Road experience, telling how he met Jesus. As he continued his story, he recalled another time the Lord—Jesus—spoke to him: "When I returned to Jerusalem and was praying at the temple, I fell into a trance and saw the Lord speaking. 'Quick!' he said to me, 'Leave Jerusalem immediately'" (22:17-18). I don't think there is any doubt that the one Paul saw was Jesus. When Paul met Him on the road to Damascus, that was who the Man said He was. It is not a stretch to conclude that when Paul prayed "Lord," he was praying to the One called Jesus (but of course, he also was speaking to God).

Is there scriptural precedence for communication with the Holy Spirit? Yes. It was the Holy Spirit who told the believers to set apart Barnabas and Saul for a special work: "While they were worshiping the Lord and fasting, the Holy Spirit said, 'Set apart for me Barnabas and Saul for the work to which I have called them.' So after they had fasted and prayed, they placed their hands on them and sent them off" (Acts 13:2-3).

The point is that early believers prayed interchangeably to the Father, Jesus, and the Holy Spirit. They knew them all as

God. They were persecuted because of their faith in Jesus; they were baptized in the Holy Spirit and received their power from Him; yet they still recognized God the Father. They did not seem to be as confused about both separating and keeping the three together as many believers are today.

What does this mean for you as you grow in prayer? My primary purpose in this chapter is to help you relax and not get bent out of shape over this complexity. You are praying to God when you pray to any of the three. There are no scriptural rules or commands that say we must pray to God the Father and only God the Father.

But, at the same time, I want to support the notion that primarily you will pray to God the Father. Why? Because we see that example most often in Scripture and because of our relationship with God. Paul wrote in Romans that when we came to Christ, we "received the Spirit of sonship. And by him we cry, 'Abba, Father.' The Spirit himself testifies with our spirit that we are God's children" (Romans 8:15-16). In Galatians, he wrote, "Because you are sons, God sent the Spirit of his Son [the Holy Spirit] into our hearts, the Spirit who calls out, 'Abba, Father'" (4:6).

We more regularly pray to the Father because of the roles of the Holy Spirit and Jesus in prayer. These verses point to the fact that it is the Holy Spirit within us that even moves us to pray, to cry, "Abba, Father." As Romans 8:26 informs us, The Holy Spirit "helps us in our weakness. We do not know what we ought to pray for, but the Spirit himself intercedes for us with groans that words cannot express." Hebrews tells us that Jesus "always lives to intercede for [believers]" (7:25). Because of our standing in Christ Jesus, because the Holy Spirit dwells within us, we can pray. We are drawn to pray.

And Jesus Himself said to pray in His name, including several times in His Last Supper discourse:

47

"I will do whatever you ask in my name, so that the Son may bring glory to the Father. You may ask me for anything in my name, and I will do it." (John 14:13-14)

"You did not choose me, but I chose you and appointed you to go and bear fruit—fruit that will last. Then the Father will give you whatever you ask in my name." (15:16)

"In that day you will no longer ask me anything. I tell you the truth, my Father will give you whatever you ask in my name. Until now you have not asked for anything in my name. Ask and you will receive, and your joy will be complete. . . . In that day you will ask in my name." (16:23-24,26)

But what does it mean to ask or to pray in Jesus' name? Books could be written on the subject, but here's a simple explanation. Because the Holy Spirit indwells us when we accept Jesus Christ as our Lord and Savior, we have the right to call God "Father". As His children, we have complete access to Him. We have the right to use Jesus' name as our authority.

Al Vander Griend explains that this means three things:

First, we are authorized to be Christ's representatives. . . . We represent him. When we stand before the throne, the Father recognizes us as persons who stand in the place of his Son. That makes us acceptable.

Second, we come to God on the basis of Christ's merit. You and I have no claim on God, but Christ does. He merited the Father's favor by his perfect life and sacrifice. When we come in Jesus' name, we are identified with him. We come on the ground of his claim on the Father.

Third, we come asking according with Christ's will. We have the mind of Christ in us, so what we ask is what he would ask. He is asking us to ask for him. We are able to ask what he would ask because our wills are in sync with his will.[1]

This means that we have an awesome responsibility. We are representing Christ—His will and wishes. That means we need to be constantly growing in His Word in order to know what His will and wishes are. We need to be always praying for God to conform us into the image of Jesus so that we will be worthy of this awesome responsibility.

"To pray in the Name of Christ," wrote Samuel Chadwick,

> is to pray as one who is at one with Christ, whose mind is the mind of Christ, whose desires are the desires of Christ, and whose purpose is one with that of Christ. . . . Prayers offered in the Name of Christ are scrutinised [sic] and sanctified by His nature, His purpose, and His will. Prayer is endorsed by the Name, when it is in harmony with the character, mind, desire, and purpose of the Name.[2]

So What?

So where does all this leave us?

First, don't worry about to whom you should pray. If at times you are led to address Jesus or the Holy Spirit, do it. For me, I often address them when what I am asking is in line with their character. For example, if someone needs comfort, I address the Comforter, the Holy Spirit. If someone needs salvation, I might address Jesus, the One whose name they must call out to.

Often those who have been believers for a while will find an aspect of God's character to address in prayer. For example, I have never heard prayer leader Evelyn Christenson pray without starting out, "Holy, Holy God." God's holiness is so meaningful to her, she comes into His presence reminding herself of it and reminding God of her respect for Him. A missionary friend of mine, Herb Lamp, finds great comfort in the fatherness of God and all that means. He almost always approaches God with "Father dear." What characteristic of God touches you? Address God with that attribute.

Second, realize that praying in Jesus' name means more than tacking "In Jesus' name, amen" onto the end of a prayer. There is authority in the name of Jesus; there is power in the name of Jesus. When we pray in His name, we are representing Him. We need to get to know Him more and more to pray effectively in His name.

Finally, even though this chapter might make you think— might make you worry—don't let it stop you from moving forward in prayer. As you grow, you will come to understand better what all this means for your prayer life. For now, remember what I said earlier in the book: Prayer is simply talking to and listening to God. It's hard to get it wrong.

For Further Reading

Praying in the Name of Jesus, Dick Eastman and Jack Hayford (Regal)

The Authority of the Believer, J. A. MacMillan (Christian Publications)

Prayer Power Unlimited, J. Oswald Sanders (Discovery House)

Attributes of God, A. W. Tozer (Christian Publications)

The Knowledge of the Holy, A. W. Tozer (HarperCollins)

Section 2

The TYPES of PRAYER

-- 5

THE PRAYER OF PETITION

M ONEY WAS TIGHT FOR ALENA AND HER HUSBAND, TEACHERS IN a Christian school. But Alena had learned the power of prayer over the years—especially in the area of financial need. She recounts one experience:

Approaching autumn two years ago [1997], my need for a warm jacket became apparent. "Lord, You know I need a jacket," I prayed. "We don't have the money to buy one."

One Saturday, my husband, Skip, and I drove leisurely up the beautiful North Cascades Highway in Washington State. We stopped at several garage sales along the way.

At Hamilton, we followed signs to a house. I sauntered up the lawn to be greeted with the words, "'Everything is free."

I scurried from table to table discovering dishes, flower pots, and many other useful items. Wreaths for my neighbor to decorate, things to give away or sell, all found their way to our van. I was nearing the end of my search, when I spotted two barrels of clothing. I pulled out a Puget Sound shirt. Then I saw it—a shiny gray, almost translucent jacket. Too big, was my initial thought, but I tried it on. It fit perfectly.

"I paid over $100 for that jacket last year," said my generous benefactor.

Excitedly I took my new jacket to the van so Skip could see my treasure. We traveled home knowing God answers prayer abundantly.

Many people compliment me on my attractive jacket. Often I say, "This jacket is an answer to prayer." Then I gratefully share how God supplied my need at a garage sale where "everything was free."

Alena's prayer was a prayer of petition. The simplest definition of petition is "a solemn, earnest request; an entreaty." When we think of petition in prayer terms, we are usually referring to a request we make for ourselves, asking God for something we need. Usually we learn the prayer of petition first. There are a number of reasons why that is true.

When we become Christians and start to pray, or even if we have been Christians a while but have never learned to pray, God wants to prove Himself to us. He wants us to realize that He hears and answers prayer. Over the years, I have been amazed at the times I have seen unusual answers to prayer in the life of a new believer. Part of this is due to the fact that a new believer's faith hasn't yet been jaded by skepticism. We tell him God answers prayer and he believes it, so he prays with faith. But most of the reason is God's desire to prove Himself faithful right away in someone's life.

We learn to pray prayers of petition first because these are the prayers that God clearly answers in our lives. Specific things we pray for ourselves—a problem at work, money to repair a car—have specific answers we can see and equate to God answering prayer.

In the introduction I shared two experiences of financial need being met as a result of prayer—furniture going on sale enough to meet my budget and extra work that raised my mortgage payment to the dollar. I have had other times where I wanted—even needed—something, prayed about it, but what I asked for never came. What made the difference? God knew I was going through a time where I needed a clear display that He was with me, that He would be all that I needed.

For some reason I, like many believers, began to pray less and less for myself. I'm not sure why. Maybe we think praying for ourselves is a sign of selfishness or immaturity. We shouldn't neglect it, however. God certainly honors such requests. "You do not have, because you do not ask God," according to James 4:2.

Even in the Lord's Prayer we are instructed to ask for ourselves: "Give us today our daily bread. Forgive us our debts, ... And lead us not into temptation, but deliver us from the evil one" (Matthew 6:11-13). These are all examples of petition—both for physical needs and spiritual ones.

—— WHAT TO ASK GOD

One of the keys to good petition is learning what to ask God. Petition can move into the realm of selfishness very quickly if all we ask for are material things beyond our basic needs. It's one thing to pray for the necessary money to cover the repairs on your only car; it's quite another to ask that you win the Publishers Clearinghouse Sweepstakes.

So what things are appropriate to ask for? Let's look at some characters from Scripture for clues.

One of the most interesting individuals in Scripture was a man named Jabez. We know absolutely nothing about him other than what is told in two verses in 1 Chronicles. What makes this intriguing is that these two verses stand out in nine chapters of solid genealogy—"The descendants of Judah:

Perez, Hezron, Carmi" and so on (1 Chronicles 4:1). Tucked in between are these words:

> *Jabez was more honorable than his brothers. His mother had named him Jabez, saying, "I gave birth to him in pain." Jabez cried out to the God of Israel, "Oh, that you would bless me and enlarge my territory! Let your hand be with me, and keep me from harm so that I will be free from pain." And God granted his request. (verses 9-10)*

Why on earth would God interrupt these genealogies with a brief picture of this obscure man? That's a good question. The Navigators prayer coordinator Lee Brase always insists on asking that question. He believes we need to look closely at the praying people in the Bible "because the prayers in the Bible represent a wide variety of prayers and fit most any situation. God has chosen to record them for us. When we look at them we need to consider what was intended when they were originally written, and why did God keep them for us today?"[1]

God was obviously pleased with Jabez's prayer. Pleased enough to make him stand out, to include him as an example for the centuries to come. "Bless me and enlarge my territory," was Jabez's request. Seems selfish. "I want more money, more power; I want to be someone." But that wasn't it. Jabez simply wanted to count for God. He wanted everything God had for him.

In his best-selling book on Jabez (that's right, an entire book on these two verses!), Dr. Bruce Wilkinson says, "To bless in the biblical sense means to ask for or to impart supernatural favor. When we ask for God's blessing, we're not asking for more of what we could get for ourselves. We're crying out for the wonderful, unlimited goodness that only God has the power to know about or give to us."[2]

There's nothing wrong with praying for that kind of blessing in our lives. God loves that kind of faith and trust. "When we seek God's blessing as the ultimate value in life," writes Wilkinson, "we are throwing ourselves entirely into the river of His will and power and purposes for us. All our other needs become secondary to what we really want—which is to become wholly immersed in what God is trying to do in us, through us, and around us for His glory."[3]

So God takes pleasure in our asking for that kind of blessing. Enough pleasure that He put Jabez's short prayer in Scripture for us to model. "We have God's permission to pray this way," writes Todd Gaddis. "In fact, we have His invitation. The imprisoned prophet Jeremiah received a challenge to do so from the Lord: 'Call to me and I will answer you and tell you great and unsearchable things you do not know.' . . . It's worth considering: What blessings might be eluding you simply because you haven't asked?"[4]

So when you petition God, ask for spiritual blessing. Ask for God's best for you. Ask to have your territory enlarged.

Another person who asked correctly was Solomon. When God told him He would grant whatever request he asked, Solomon replied,

> *"You have shown great kindness to David my father and have made me king in his place. Now, LORD God, let your promise to my father David be confirmed, for you have made me king over a people who are as numerous as the dust of the earth. Give me* wisdom and knowledge, *that I may lead this people, for who is able to govern this great people of yours?" (2 Chronicles 1:8-10, emphasis added)*

Of all the things he could have asked for, Solomon chose something that pleased God. And God said to Solomon,

*"Since this is your heart's desire and you have not asked
for wealth, riches or honor, nor for the death of your enemies, and since you have not asked for a long life but for
wisdom and knowledge to govern my people over whom I
have made you king, therefore wisdom and knowledge will
be given you. And I will also give you wealth, riches and
honor, such as no king who was before you ever had and
none after you will have."* (verses 11-12)

Solomon became the richest, most powerful, most suc-
cessful king in Israel's history. He was world renowned for his
wisdom. An interesting side note to this prayer: though God
didn't mention this, Solomon was also the only king in Israel's
history who enjoyed peace throughout his reign. How's that
for blessing!

So What?

Okay, you may be thinking, *you've convinced me. It's all right to
pray for blessing. I can pray for myself without thinking I'm selfish.
But what should I pray?*

Start by asking for things that you know are God's will for
you to have. Things like the fruit of the Spirit, Christlikeness.
"How much more will your Father in heaven give good gifts to
those who ask him!" (Matthew 7:11). Ask for those good gifts,
says Al Vander Griend: "The 'good things' Jesus had in mind
are the spiritual blessings of grace, wisdom, joy, peace, power,
holiness, and so on. These are things in accord with God's will.
We can ask the Father for them with absolute assurance that he
will give them to us. It's what he has promised."[5]

Are there areas of your life that you know are sin or out of
God's will? Pray for God to move in those areas. Are there
weaknesses in your character? Pray for God's transformation.
Do you want your life to amount to something for God? Then,

if you are willing to take the exciting ride, ask for God's blessing. Ask and ask and ask.

For Further Reading

"Dare to Pray the Jabez Way!" Todd Gaddis (*Pray!* Issue 15, November/December 1999)
The Prayer of Jabez, Dr. Bruce Wilkinson (Multnomah)

— 6

THE PRAYER OF INTERCESSION

"SIMON, SIMON," JESUS SAID TO PETER, "SATAN HAS ASKED TO sift you as wheat. But I have prayed for you, Simon, that your faith may not fail. And when you have turned back, strengthen your brothers" (Luke 22:31-32).

The stage was set. Jesus was nearing the cross. Lost in the story leading to Calvary lies this valuable prayer lesson. Hidden away in one verse in Luke, Jesus gives us a powerful picture of intercession. Peter, still brave and boasting, was taught a simple truth about the in-workings of the spirit realm.

The picture here is almost of a heavenly court. Satan asked God's permission to attack Peter; Jesus pleaded Peter's case before the Father. That's a portrait of intercession.

—— THE HEAVENLY COURT

Prayer leader Steve Hawthorne tells of a time when he had the opportunity to help a friend in a court case. His friend was a Chinese student studying in America. Though this student could read and write English fairly well, speaking spontaneously was tough for him.

Once, after being taken advantage of by an auto mechanic, the student decided to take the man to small claims court. Because he had trouble speaking, he asked Steve if he would speak for him before the judge. Steve agreed.

The day in court came. Steve got up to speak, but the judge cut him off. "Are you an attorney?" he asked Steve. When Steve revealed that he wasn't, but was merely speaking on behalf of his Chinese friend, the judge informed him that the man would have to speak for himself. He did—in fluent Mandarin. The judge threw out the case.

Steve related that some time afterward, as he was praying for China, his friend and the court case came to mind. The next thing Steve knew, he envisioned himself and his friend standing in a heavenly court, before God. Steve began passionately pleading his friend's case—for salvation—before God.

That's a very real picture of intercession. The Bible is full of illustrations that speak of a heavenly court, of some kind of interaction that takes place in God's presence. This passage in Luke 22 is just one example. Another well-known example begins the book of Job, when Satan asks God's permission to attack Job to prove that if the going got tough, Job would curse God.

When we pray on behalf of others, we are in a sense entering an exchange in a heavenly throne room. From that idea, we get the word *intercession* to describe a type of prayer. Webster's dictionary defines *intercede* as "pleading in behalf of another, or mediating."

All the uses of intercede, intercessor, and intercession in Scripture seem to point this out—especially when we compare the King James Version to modern translations. Consider Isaiah 59:16. The King James translates it as "he saw that there was no man, and wondered that there was no *intercessor*" (emphasis added). The New International Version translates the verse, "He saw that there was no one, he was appalled that there was no one to *intervene*"(emphasis added). A little earlier, in Isaiah's great prophetic chapter about Christ, he said this of Jesus, "For he bore the sin of many, and made intercession for the transgressors" (53:12). The meaning of intercession in both verses seems to be "go-between" or "stand-in"—almost the idea of mediating for someone. Jesus, on the cross, stood in for sinners—He interceded for us.

Jeremiah 7:16 and Romans 11:2 offer a slightly different twist on the word, but retain the sense of being in court. "So do not pray for this people nor offer any plea or petition for them; do not *plead* with me, for I will not listen" (Jeremiah 7:16, NIV, emphasis added). The King James puts it, "neither make *intercession* to me" (emphasis added). Paul, speaking of Elijah, said, "Don't you know what the Scripture says in the passage about Elijah—how he appealed to God against Israel" (Romans 11:2, NIV). The King James uses *intercession* instead of *appeal*.

You get the idea. When we are interceding for someone, we are pleading a case, appealing to God on behalf of the situation.

But what does that mean for us as we learn to pray?

First, in a very real way, we need to look at intercession with passion, with a sense that our prayers could make the difference between "winning and losing." Too often, when we are asked to pray for something, we come at it with a lackluster, ho-hum attitude: *My prayers won't matter in this situation; surely others are praying too.* Or we believe that God is going to do His will in this situation regardless of whether or not we pray, so we are not burdened to pray. Nothing could be further from the truth.

"Our Western mindset," says Hawthorne,

> tells us "What does it really matter if I say words into the air?" Or "If God knows what He's going to do, why doesn't He just do it?" But if God truly presides as Judge, with His court ever in session (Genesis 18:20-23; Psalm 65:1-4;

Hebrews 4:14-16, 7:25-8:2), our words of intercession are not just sound waves hitting the ceiling. Our expressions of prayer reverberate throughout God's court, not just for Him to hear, but for all the angelic hosts before whom this awesome drama is being played out.[1]

Scripture also clearly indicates that intercession is important to God. How do we know this? Because both the Holy Spirit and Jesus are involved. Romans 8 tells us that "the Spirit himself intercedes for us with groans that words cannot express. . . . The Spirit intercedes for the saints in accordance with God's will" (verses 26-27); and "Christ Jesus, who died—more than that, who was raised to life—is at the right hand of God and is also interceding for us" (verse 34). Hebrews reminds us that "[Jesus] is able to save completely those who come to God through him, because he always lives to intercede for them" (Hebrews 7:25).

We need to attack every situation we feel a tug to pray about as if we were the only one praying! You might be the only person who ever prays for your unbelieving neighbor's salvation. No praying grandmother. No Christian wife praying for her husband. No believer at work. Only you.

—— THE POWER OF A BURDEN

As you grow in intercession you will soon learn about burdens. While we all will have those people for whom we regularly intercede—perhaps our children, parents, spouse, pastor, friends—from time to time God will place "a prayer burden" on you. A prayer burden is simply when an unusual tug to pray for a specific person or situation comes upon you. It may come during your regular prayer time. Perhaps as you are interceding for your daughter away at college, a strong urge to keep praying for her—often regarding a specific issue or circumstance (maybe protection)—comes upon you. You cannot seem to stop praying, so you keep at it until the feeling lifts.

Other times, a prayer burden will come on you at an unusual time. (God often wakes up believers in the middle of the night and puts the name or picture of a specific person in their minds.) You may think it odd because you rarely, or never, think about that person. When that happens, God is prompting you to intercede for that person because he or she is greatly in need of prayer at that moment or soon will be. On a number of occasions I have had intercessor friends call me and say, "I was burdened to pray for you yesterday morning at nine. What happened?" Once I had been in a very important meeting, the decisions of which would have ramifications for *Pray!* Other times I did not see a correlation to their burden, but who knows what I was protected from by their prayers.

In her book *Intercession, Thrilling and Fulfilling,* Joy Dawson tells the story of a friend, Len Ravenhill, who had a powerful prayer burden. Len and his wife, Martha, were awakened one night at midnight by three knocks on their bedroom door. No one was there. Sensing the need to pray for his three sons, who were in various parts of the world, Len did so and went back to bed. At exactly 4 A.M. the knocks came again. Again no one was there. Len prayed fervently for his sons and their families. He prayed until peace came. A few days later a letter arrived from their son David, who lived in California.

> On exactly the same night that Len and Martha had been awakened, David and his wife Nancy were awakened at midnight with the noise from several fire trucks and firemen putting out a fire in the house next door. When they saw that the fire was under control, they went back to bed and to sleep.

At 4 A.M., they were awakened by someone knocking on their front door. When they opened it, a nice-looking man told them about a fire in the house next door that was raging out of control. The stranger urged them to get out of their house, as the tops of the trees that separated them from their neighbor were already burning. David called the fire department while Nancy grabbed their baby and the man carried their four-year-old daughter. As they walked across the street to safety, Nancy looked up into the dark sky and to her amazement saw a sentence written in red: "Your house will be saved."

The fire trucks were delayed in coming, and it looked impossible to save the house. While David tried desperately to get help from the neighbors, the stranger calmly announced to Nancy that no further help was needed. A police car then arrived and radioed for help, and finally the fire trucks came. In the nick of time, the house was saved.

David took their four-year-old daughter from the man who had been holding her. Then, just as David and Nancy were about to thank him for warning them about the danger, the man disappeared. He was nowhere to be seen. Shaken but profoundly grateful, the couple returned with their children to their unharmed home with a strong sense of the pervading presence of the Lord.[2]

Don't ignore a burden when it comes. God placed it upon you because, to release His will, He needs your prayers (see chapter 1).

Many believers also have another type of prayer burden operating in their life of intercession. As you grow in your prayer life, it is very likely that you will find one or two prayer concerns that excite you when you intercede for them. For example, you may get excited when you pray for revival in the church, or maybe it's when you pray for missionaries, or abused women, or your pastor, or pastors in general. This represents another prayer burden. For many, God will place a calling on their lives to focus a great deal of time lifting up a specific issue.

When this kind of burden begins to come on you, I have two words of challenge. First, never demand that your burden become other people's burden too. If God leads you to set up a prayer meeting to pray for your burden or to find some prayer partners to pray with you, wonderful. But don't get discouraged if others do not join you. And don't force them or try to make them feel guilty. God gives each of us different burdens. Your burden is no more or less important than anyone else's. Second, do everything you can to fuel your burden with truth. By that I mean, get information about your burden. Do research, read. Find out some facts. If it is a specific person, try to find out things that you can pray about, without being nosy in the process. Our church has a program in which intercessors pray for a specific child in the congregation. Often these intercessors will ask parents (or the child herself), "What's happening in her life? What are some specific things I can pray for her?"

—— A Calling

Finally, as you grow in prayer, you may eventually find you have a calling to intercession itself. What do I mean by that? There are certain people who God seems to specially grace with the desire to pray for hours a day on behalf of others. While we may struggle to stay focused in prayer for ten to fifteen minutes, these choice pray-ers seem to effortlessly spend hours at a time pleading cases before the throne.

My assistant, Sandie, is such a person. She would rather be in her prayer closet than anywhere else! As a result, she has a rich relationship with God. She seems to hear from God far more than I or most believers do. And her prayers are answered—sometimes in absolutely amazing ways. But she pays a price that most of us do not want to pay. Those called to intercession are often misunderstood. Sometimes they are grieved by others who do not receive kindly God's word to them or who are upset by what God leads these intercessors to pray in a situation. While Sandie is one of the humblest people I know, many are intimidated by her, perhaps thinking she believes she is more spiritual because of the amount of time she spends in prayer. That couldn't be further from the truth!

If you begin to sense God calling you to this ministry, here are some tips:

Find another intercessor to mentor you. Make sure it is someone who has a good relationship with his or her pastor and church. Sometimes intercessors can become withdrawn and even critical of their church. That is not healthy; and you do not want to be mentored by someone like that.

Make sure you spend time in the Word. As you begin to spend long times in prayer, reading and meditating on God's Word will help you stay balanced. Intercessors who are not grounded in God's Word quickly become targets that Satan can manipulate for his purposes. Never pray at length without an open Bible. Pray the Word (see chapter 10).

Guard against a prideful spirit. One of Satan's best tactics for destroying intercessors is to fill them with pride. You may start to feel more spiritual than others. You may start to get annoyed that your church "isn't doing things right." These are signs of pride creeping in. Pride will totally invalidate your ministry!

Develop your calling. Read books about intercessors and intercession. Fill your prayer closet with things that stimulate your prayer life: maps, photographs, powerful quotes, and the like.

So What?

By now you may be saying, "I'm not at that level! Where do I start?" Start the same way I suggested in chapter 2. Pick a few things outside your own needs for which to begin interceding. Start with areas or people that you feel some passion about. Perhaps it is your children or spouse, maybe your church or pastor, maybe the salvation of a neighbor or coworker. Once focused on the issues you feel led to pray about, begin seeking God as to how to pray for them. Do some fact-finding, if appropriate. If you are praying for your church or pastor, ask for requests. Where do they think they need prayer? Ask God for specific Scriptures to pray.

If you have access to the Internet, click on "Prayer Points" at www.nationalprayer.org. This site provides suggestions of how to pray for certain items or situations. You'll find prayer points based on Scripture to pray for your children, your pastors, your neighbors, those in authority, missionaries, even specific nations.

Keep lists in your Bible. Perhaps keep a journal where you can write down what you are praying for, what God is saying to you about that issue/person, and when the prayers were answered.

Is intercession powerful? Yes. When I was going through the breakup of my marriage thirteen years ago, my mom went to prayer. We were part of a small denomination. Because my grandfather had been a pastor in the denomination, my dad and one brother were current pastors, and my other brother worked at the denomination's national office, news got around. In a conservative denomination like ours, many ministry doors would shut for me because of my being divorced.

My mom began praying that, eventually, knowledge of the glory that my life brought to God would spread further than the knowledge of my broken marriage. What happened? In 1989 I went into publishing at my denomination's publishing house. Eventually, three books of mine were published. I became managing editor of *Discipleship Journal*, which reaches more than 100,000 readers each issue. God used me to found *Pray!* magazine. He has given me the opportunity to speak around the country. God truly has blessed my life in amazing ways, despite the broken marriage and the pain I went through. I am humbled that He has allowed me the privilege to minister in those ways for His kingdom.

All this happened without my knowledge of my mother's intercession. Mom told me of her persistent prayers on my behalf the day before my first television appearance, on a talk show that would air across the United States. Yes, intercession works! Start interceding!

For Further Reading

Intercession, Thrilling and Fulfilling, Joy Dawson (YWAM Publishing)
Intercessory Prayer, Dutch Sheets (Regal)
Love on Its Knees, Dick Eastman (Baker)
Prayer: The Great Adventure, David Jeremiah (Multnomah)

— 7

HEARING GOD'S VOICE

FRUSTRATED. THAT'S THE BEST WORD TO DESCRIBE MY FEELINGS. I had left a job I loved, feeling strongly led by God to do so. But here I was, three months later, questioning whether or not I had made a mistake.

I had been the head of the editorial department of Christian Publications during a period when we had gone from publishing nine books a year to forty. It had been exciting! But busy. I had been overworked, often putting in fifty- to sixty-hour weeks. When the inquiry came from NavPress about becoming managing editor of *Discipleship Journal*, something within me was drawn to the position.

When offered the job, I prayed about it and sought the counsel of respected friends. I weighed the pros and cons. After all that, I felt very confident that it was God's will for me.

Now here I was, three months later, feeling like I had made a mistake. Had I been wrong in trying to discern God's will? Was my frustration just a carnal thing—I was no longer in charge of a department, didn't have a secretary or a private office, and the pace of work was much slower (something I don't like). Or was the anxiety a combination of the two?

I began questioning God in my prayers: *Should I look for another job in the area? Was that why You brought me to Colorado Springs?* I needed answers.

One evening, while working on a freelance editing job for my former employer, I had an unusual experience. I was updating a classic book, *In the School of Faith,* by A. B. Simpson. Concentrating on the project before me, I wasn't thinking at all about my job situation. As I came to Simpson's commentary on Esther 4:14 — "who knoweth whether thou art come to the kingdom for such a time as this" (KJV) — a very distinct and clear thought entered my mind out of the blue: "I brought you here for something else."

Instantly my mind was alert. *What was that?* I thought. "I brought you here for something else." I immediately went to prayer. I knew it had been the voice of God and I knew it was about my job situation, not simply my mind wandering as I thought about Esther. As I prayed—and listened—I became convinced that God had a purpose for bringing me to Colorado Springs, that it would be at NavPress, but that *Discipleship Journal* was only a stepping-stone to something else God ultimately had planned.

Hearing God's voice that night was enough to ease my frustration and put me at peace with my job situation. But it also put me on the alert, watching for what God had for me. Interestingly, I never heard God speak to me again regarding that issue, or speak directly about why He had brought me to Colorado Springs. But as I look back now I can clearly see His hand.

Four months later, as I was sitting on a plane flying to New York, yet another thought came to me out of the blue. This one, however, did not feel like the voice of God, but rather the mental wanderings of a bored airplane passenger trying to pass the time. I remember thinking about the growing prayer movement, different things I was seeing and wanted to be a part of.

Suddenly I thought, *Wouldn't a magazine on prayer, a voice for the prayer movement, be an interesting thing to produce?* I knew the NavPress periodicals division was looking for new products to develop, so why not a small magazine on prayer? After pondering the idea for a while, I decided, *Nah, a magazine on one aspect of the Christian life? It'll never make it.* And I forgot about it.

But it turned out to be an idea that wouldn't go away. My mind would turn toward it when I was daydreaming. I would awaken in the middle of the night thinking about what the magazine would look like, who would be involved, and so on. Details came to me at the oddest times.

Finally in January 1995 I presented the idea to my boss. Thus began the journey toward *Pray!* magazine—what God had purposely brought me to Colorado Springs to do. Over the next two years of developing *Pray!*, things did not go easily. Needed funds weren't coming in. A new boss was hesitant to start a risky venture as the first thing on his watch. A financial deadline to stop development was looming. Did my faith waver? A little in the down moments, but I can honestly say that God's words to me back in July 1994 were sufficient to carry me through. The strong memory of His voice gave me two years of calm assurance that this matter was in His hands and He was going to bring it about.

—— DOES GOD SPEAK?

Unfortunately many churches today teach that God speaks only through the Bible. That teaching comes out of a fear of excess. Many have seen others abuse authority and power by saying, "God told me that you (or we) should (fill in the blank)." Or they've seen people who put as much weight on what they thought they heard God saying to them as they did on Scripture. Both of those criticisms are accurate. People often do both of those things. But you do not throw out something clearly taught in Scripture (the fact that God speaks to His followers) because of a few people's abuses.

Writing on this topic, prayer leader Timothy Jones comments,

> Some Christians conclude that God said all that needed saying 2,000 years ago. He stopped talking much when Jesus ascended and the Bible was compiled. Our listening, they argue, should be confined to what we read in Scripture. Perhaps, they allow, God communicates through ethical principles or a pastor or religious leader. But a specific, personal word? That smacks of mysticism or wishful thinking.[1]

I am confident in telling you that God does indeed speak today! Both experience and Scripture bear this out. In John 10:27, Jesus said, "My sheep *listen* to my voice; I know them, and they follow me" (emphasis added). Earlier in that chapter, speaking of natural sheep and the shepherd, Jesus said, "The sheep listen to [the shepherd's] voice" (verse 3). God told Isaiah "Whether you turn to the right or to the left, *your ears will hear* a voice behind you, saying, 'This is the way; walk in it'" (Isaiah 30:21, emphasis added). The indication is that communication—through speaking and hearing—will take place between God and His followers. As you grow in your prayer life and learn some listening skills, you will hear God talking to you.

But how do you learn to hear and what do you do with what you hear?

— GETTING THE WAX OUT

The first step toward learning to hear God speak is to spend time with Him. Make sure you are reading Scripture, meditating on it, and spending time with God in prayer—both speaking to Him and listening. You will develop your sense of hearing as you use it.

While I did say that God speaks today—and I believe He will speak even when you are not sitting with an open Bible in your lap—I also believe the primary place He does speak is through Scripture. You will most likely first develop your ear for His voice as you read the Bible. A verse will stand out to you. As you meditate upon it (think about it), you may hear "you need to apply that to _____ situation," and your mind begins to think about the situation with clarity. That was God's voice.

You also need to be reading Scripture to put God's Word in your heart. The psalmist said, "I have hidden your word in my heart that I might not sin against you" (Psalm 119:11). A little later in the chapter he wrote, "Your word is a lamp to my feet and a light for my path" (verse 105). If you are practicing listening and want to hear God's voice, you must be reading and memorizing Scripture constantly. The reason? What God says to you will never violate Scripture. For example, if you were having trouble in your marriage, God's voice would never tell you it's okay to have an affair with someone else or to divorce your wife. That "word" clearly is opposite of what Scripture says about adultery and divorce. That voice is simply your own flesh talking—or Satan. The more you know Scripture, the easier you can quickly dismiss outside voices as not being from God.

Indeed, the biggest problem in hearing God's voice is discerning between His voice, the voice of our own flesh, and Satan's voice. Gaining more and more knowledge of Scripture helps us to discern the difference. But so does spending time with God in prayer. You will learn to recognize His voice the more you hear it.

The boy Samuel in the Old Testament shows us this truth. One night as he was trying to sleep, he heard someone call his name, "Samuel, Samuel." He ran to Eli, his mentor, saying, "Here I am." But Eli told Samuel he hadn't called. This happened three times before Eli realized the Lord was speaking to

Samuel. So he told the boy to say, "Speak, LORD, for your servant is listening," the next time the voice called out (1 Samuel 3). In the midst of these verses lies a telling fact: "Now Samuel did not yet know the LORD: The word of the LORD had not yet been revealed to him" (1 Samuel 3:7).

That may be the case for many of us. We have not yet heard the Lord, so we find it difficult to discern His voice. The last verses in the chapter give a different picture of Samuel's life: "The LORD was with Samuel as he grew up, and he let none of his words fall to the ground. And all Israel from Dan to Beersheba recognized that Samuel was attested as a prophet of the LORD. The LORD continued to appear at Shiloh, and there he revealed himself to Samuel through his word" (1 Samuel 3:19-21). Wouldn't it be great to have the same thing said of our lives at the end — that none of God's words fell to the ground. The more we listen, the more we will discern.

Teaching pastor Eric Simpson of Eagle Church in Indianapolis gave this excellent illustration about recognizing God's voice. He and his wife had recently had their first baby, Lilly. Eric was present in the birthing room. When Lilly was born by C-section, she was immediately whisked away to another part of the room to be cared for. Even though people all around Lilly were talking and shouting out instructions, when Eric said, "Hi, Lilly; it's your daddy," she immediately turned her head toward his voice. She had picked out one of the two voices she had been hearing over the past nine months. She was familiar with it, so she turned toward it. That's the way we should eventually be with God's voice, if we listen, discern, and practice listening.

Author Marilyn Heavilin offers five principles to remember as we seek to discern what words are God's and what words are not.

1. *Christ convicts; Satan condemns.* Is the voice you are hearing condemning or simply lovingly convicting? "There is now no condemnation for those who are in Christ Jesus" (Romans 8:1). Satan is the "accuser of [the] brethren" (Revelation 12:10, KJV). Heavilin writes, "When I hear the voice of condemnation, I try to remind myself that God loathes sin but loves me and would never declare me worthless. Then I give my favorite order to Satan: 'Scram!' It works every time."[2]

2. Christ clarifies; Satan confuses. Satan will try to confuse us with the world's philosophy. He will try to *twist* Scripture: "That can't really be what God is saying." Our protection will be to seek God and to spend time in His Word. Heavilin advises, "Pray that [God] will give [you] a sound mind and protect [you] from confusion as [you] listen for His voice."[3]

3. Christ confirms; Satan contradicts. God never contradicts His Word, the Bible. "Satan, however," says Heavilin, "will arrange circumstances to look like we are experiencing divine intervention in an attempt to blind us to contradictions to God's truth."[4]

4. Christ chooses; Satan captures. Satan delights in tripping us. When he comes to us, he will put subtle thoughts into our hearts that it is okay to do something we know is contrary to God's Word. Christ chose us with no strings attached. His voice will be loving, pointing us to the truth.

5. Christ compels; Satan constricts. God's voice will be constantly moving us forward, taking us deeper *into* our relationship with Him. It will compel us to seek truth. Satan's voice will constantly put rebellious thoughts into our hearts: *Is that what God really said?*

Again, how do we discern God's voice? Spend time with Him in prayer and reading His Word.

—— WHAT IF I HEAR SOMETHING?

One of the most controversial issues in the church today falls in the arena of the "prophetic word." While this terminology can mean different things to different believers, for this book I am defining it as *hearing God telling you something about someone else or about a church or situation.* Perhaps nowhere else in the church is more damage done or more abuse perpetrated than here. For that reason, I have some extremely strong warnings and cautions.

I personally believe God does speak today and He does give insights to people—especially through prayer—regarding situations. But because of the dangers of hearing wrong, I am not in the camp that thinks this ability should be sought. In most cases, if God does give you insight, it is meant so you can pray with knowledge about the situation, not so you can tell others what to do, or worse, presume to tell them what God wants them to do. Horror stories abound about some "prophet" who told a church or individual that God wanted something done, only to have it cause awful damage. Hurt and destruction can occur because so often the word was not from God, or the intercessor interpreted it incorrectly, or the word was from God but it was not meant to be shared.

In my own life, I can think of a number of significant times when I heard direction regarding a situation. Not once did I feel compelled to share what I had heard to the person involved or to the decision makers in the situation.

One of the times came when I was praying for a friend of mine who has a debilitating illness. Bill (not his real name) had struggled with the disease for years, yet he felt God had spoken to him that he would eventually be healed. I have prayed a lot—in faith—for Bill. This particular day—and numerous times since—as I was praying, the word *bitterness* came to me. In the days that followed, I felt with increasing clarity that a wall of bitterness existed within Bill's life and family. I started focusing on that in my prayers for Bill.

Now, I could have—as many intercessors do—gone right to Bill and confronted him with this word. But I felt no such compulsion. Had I done so and been wrong—or been right but Bill was not ready to receive it—it would have created spiritual havoc in Bill's life, anger at me, turmoil. God only gave me insight into how to pray for Bill; He did not give me authority over Bill's life to challenge him. God is fully capable of revealing the problem to Bill in His time; He doesn't need me to do it for Him.

I would never tell someone unless I had an extreme burden or compulsion to do so—and only after a great deal of prayer.

I have also had times in my life when intercessors have shared something with me that God had shared with them. Both times, however, God used them to confirm something I was already pondering. They brought confirmation and encouragement, not turmoil and confusion.

In January 1999, while at a nationwide gathering of prayer leaders, I had my first such experience. We were in the middle of a worship time late Saturday afternoon when Beth Alves, a woman who I knew of but had never met or spoken to in my life, came up to me. She told me God had said that I was thinking of a partnership with another organization and that He wanted me to know that the partnership was of Him.

That got my attention! Unbeknown to Beth, I had only the day before been talking to George Otis Jr. regarding a publication his ministry was producing. During the conversation, the idea of a possible partnership came up, but I didn't pursue it, because I thought it would never fly with my superiors. Yet Beth's word encouraged me. When I got back to work, I presented the idea to my boss—without telling him what happened at my meeting. I figured if God was in this, He would break down the barriers. To my shock, my boss was for it. After the decisions had been made, I told him about Beth's word.

My point? If you truly hear from God regarding something, you do not need to force anything. Simply be obedient to what

God may be leading you to do—or more likely, leading you to pray—and let Him do the rest. I did not need to push anything with that partnership. I did not need to use the clout of "God told me to." Because I stayed in prayer and kept moving through open doors, His will came about. Beth's word gave me confidence and peace that we were doing the right thing.

So What?

In closing, let me review the key points regarding hearing from God.

First, if you are a believer, you *should* hear God's voice, though likely not in dramatic fashion. It will come as you meditate on Scripture, as you seek to find His will in a situation. It may come as a verse standing out to you, giving you insight into what to do. It may come as an "unusual prompting." (Intercessor Rebecca Livermore tells the story of a friend who felt a prompting to go to the grocery store and buy potatoes. She didn't need any potatoes! But the prompting was strong, and she obeyed. While Rebecca's friend was sheepishly scrutinizing the potatoes, a woman came up to her. She led her to Christ in the produce aisle![5]) It may simply come as a gentle "I love you," a peace that you are God's child.

Second, if while praying for someone or something, you gain an insight into the situation, use it to pray more intelligently. That insight is not license to share the information with the person or with others. Sharing should only be done if you feel an absolutely clear sense to do so following much prayer.

Third, spend time in God's Word. God's voice will never violate His written Word. You will not have the ability to discern correctly if you do not have a solid understanding of the Bible. Start a systematic reading plan to read through the Bible in a year or two.

Finally, keep the lines of communication open between you

and God. Deal quickly with sin, and continually ask the Holy Spirit to search your heart. Ask God to increase your hunger to know Him. If you are doing these things regularly, Satan cannot gain a foothold in your heart to deceive you.

For Further Reading

"Are You Listening: Tuning In to God's Voice" (*Pray!* Issue 13, July/August 1999)
I'm Listening, Lord, Marilyn Heavilin (Thomas Nelson)
21 Days to a Better Quiet Time, Timothy Jones (Zondervan)
Listening to God, Jan Johnson (NavPress)

— 8

PRAYERS OF ADORATION
AND THANKSGIVING

O NE OF MY PEEVES WHEN I LEAD A PRAYER GROUP IS HOW OFTEN
people who've been asked to start our time with praise
and adoration—exalting God for who He is—quickly fall into
prayers thanking Him for what He has done.

It frustrates me for a number of reasons. I wonder, do
people not know the difference between adoration and thanksgiving? Or is the problem related to self? We find it easy to focus
on what God has done for us—things that have benefited us—
but more difficult to simply adore God for who He is. For most
of us, especially men, intimacy doesn't come easy. We find it difficult to praise someone just for who they are or for the quality
of something they did. Thanks comes much easier.

Writer Joan Esherick commented on this struggle in her
own prayer group:

> We were instructed to set aside certain amounts of time for
> adoration, confession, thanksgiving, and intercession. Almost
> immediately, however, our prayers of adoration were dis-
> placed by thanksgiving for things God had done. There was

hardly any time spent delighting in who God is, no expressions of love for Him, and little praise for His character. We were so focused on His action that we failed to worship and adore His person.[1]

But does this distinction in prayer really matter? Should I get bent out of shape over it? Well, perhaps I don't need to get bent out of shape, but yes, it does matter. It matters because praise and adoration are powerful weapons of warfare. It matters because adoration comes from a deeper level of intimacy than thankfulness. As a spouse, I get much more pleasure from my wife saying, "Jon, I love you," than from her saying, "Thanks for doing the dishes." While I enjoy receiving a pat on the back for what I do, it is much more meaningful when I know I am simply appreciated, accepted, and loved for who I am.

The psalmists recognized this truth. While there are plenty of lines of thanksgiving within the Psalms, adoration seems to take center stage:

> *Praise the* LORD, *O my soul;*
> *all my inmost being, praise his holy name. (103:1)*

> *The* LORD *reigns, he is robed in majesty;*
> *the* LORD *is robed in majesty*
> *and is armed with strength.*
> *The world is firmly established;*
> *it cannot be moved.*
> *Your throne was established long ago;*
> *you are from all eternity. (93:1-2)*

> *Shout with joy to God, all the earth!*
> *Sing the glory of his name;*
> *make his praise glorious!*

Say to God, "How awesome are your deeds!
So great is your power
that your enemies cringe before you.
All the earth bows down to you;
they sing praise to you,
they sing praise to your name." (66:1-4)

Most prayer format acronyms have both adoration and thanksgiving as important aspects of prayer. The most common one, ACTS (Adoration, Confession, Thanksgiving, Supplication), starts with adoration. But why is it important to differentiate between them? Why should both be a regular part of one's prayer life?

⸺ THE IMPORTANCE OF ADORATION

Learning to express adoration to God is important for a number of reasons.

First, it puts things into perspective. When we start adoring God, recognizing who He is, mulling over the meanings of His attributes as we offer them up in prayer, our problems and needs reduce in importance. Our faith in God's abilities to do what's best for us rises when we praise Him. Speaking of this fact in his book *The Art of Prayer,* Timothy Jones writes,

> What is the chief end of humankind? asks a venerable Scottish catechism. Schoolchildren for generations have learned the concise answer: "To glorify God and enjoy him forever." Significant things happen when we simply gaze in God's direction. Our desperately urgent agendas may wane, our concerns about our world paling next to the One who inhabits heaven. We learn simply to take pleasure in a great and wonderful God.[2]

A number of prayers recorded in Scripture follow the pattern of starting with adoration or praise. It was almost as if the pray-er was reminding God of who He is.

Peter and John, when threatened with their lives if they continued to speak of Jesus Christ, prayed this way:

"Sovereign Lord . . . you made the heaven and the earth and the sea, and everything in them. You spoke by the Holy Spirit through the mouth of your servant, our father David:

> *"'Why do the nations rage*
> *and the peoples plot in vain?*
> *The kings of the earth take their stand*
> *and the rulers gather together*
> *against the Lord*
> *and against his Anointed One.'*

"Indeed Herod and Pontius Pilot met together with the Gentiles and the people of Israel in this city [Jerusalem] to conspire against your holy servant, Jesus, whom you anointed. They did what your power and will had decided beforehand should happen. Now, Lord, consider their threats and enable your servants to speak your word with great boldness. Stretch out your hand to heal and perform miraculous signs and wonders through the name of your holy servant, Jesus." (Acts 4:24-30)

Their recognition of God's might seemed to bolster their faith to ask for boldness. They reminded God—and themselves—of His sovereignty. This gave them some perspective about their situation as they realized that in spite of their persecution, God was in control and He would work miracles.

Jeremiah provides another example of the importance of adoration. The prophet's prayer recorded in Jeremiah 32 came at a time of extreme distress. He was being held captive by King Zedekiah in the royal palace in Judah for delivering unpopular prophecies. An enemy was about to overrun the city and drag the people off into captivity in Babylon. In the midst of this, God told Jeremiah to buy a plot of land as a symbol that He would eventually restore the people to their land. Seen in the light of all his problems, Jeremiah's prayer is astounding.

He began with praise: "Ah, Sovereign LORD, you have made the heavens and the earth by your great power and out-stretched arm. Nothing is too hard for you. . . . O great and powerful God, whose name is the LORD Almighty, great are your purposes and mighty are your deeds" (Jeremiah 32:17-19). He then went on and on, simply naming various deeds God had done for Israel over the centuries. The amazing realization: Jeremiah never asked God for a thing! "Jeremiah tuned his heart to God by talking to Him," comments Lee Brase. "Through this process of talking to God, Jeremiah was able to come to a clearer understanding of Him. When he better understood God, he was able to accept what God was doing—even though it was devastating."[3]

Adoration, in a very real way, helps us to trust in God. When we remind God of His character, of how great He is, of who He is, we are also reminding ourselves of those things. Our love for God increases, and our faith to believe He can and will act in our lives rises to a higher level.

Second, adoration and praise develop within us a deeper sense of intimacy. When we voice thoughts of praise and adoration to God, we are drawn into His presence. Our praises set the tone for intimate contact with almighty God.

Psalm 22:3 says that God "inhabits" the praises of His people. Jack Hayford tells us,

The Hebrew word for "inhabit" may also be translated "enthroned," opening the passage to show us its meaning: God creates a dwelling place among those who praise Him. . . . Here is a magnificent truth! Just as God is sovereign whether we worship Him or not, He will indwell us mightily and majestically whether we are feeling happy or sad—when we praise Him. Praise constructs a Throne room in our hearts where the Sovereign God declares He is pleased to dwell.[4]

In my own prayer life, when I start with adoration and praise, I know something happens. I have a greater sense that I am connecting with God, more of a sense that He is there with me. And it is generally true that the longer I worship Him, the more powerful my prayer time is. Sometimes I'll play a worship CD to aid me. I sing along with it or simply meditate on the lyrics as they are sung. It never ceases to bring peace to my spirit and to create love for God in my heart. I have to admit that, despite knowing this, I often rush right into petition. Perhaps it is my busyness, perhaps it is my selfishness (I must get right away to what I need), or perhaps it is a fear of intimacy. Whatever the reason, I need to constantly remind myself to simply worship God in prayer. It makes all the difference!

Finally, adoration and praise are powerful spiritual warfare weapons. Satan hates it when we praise God. Why? Because he wants to be worshiped instead! When we worship God, Satan runs. Psalm 8:2 tells us, "From the lips of children and infants you have ordained praise because of your enemies, to silence the foe and the avenger." When we praise God, the enemy is silenced! Psalm 149:6-9 indicates that praise in our mouths works to "inflict vengeance on the nations and punishment on the peoples, to bind their kings with fetters, their nobles with shackles of iron. . . . This is the glory of all his saints."

Second Chronicles 20 contains an amazing story of the power of praise. When faced with a powerful enemy—too powerful for his armies—King Jehoshaphat called for a time of fasting and prayer during which God revealed He would bring victory. Somehow Jehoshaphat got the crazy idea (it had to come from God) to march against these armies with singers in the front of his army. The singers lifted beautiful praises to God: "Give thanks to the LORD, for his love endures forever" (20:21). The result? The opposing armies began attacking each other. The army of Judah didn't even have to fight! That's the power of praise! Make it a regular part of your prayer life.

—— WHAT ABOUT THANKSGIVING?

Thanksgiving is also an important component of prayer. As you develop in your prayer life, you need to continually remind yourself of what God has done for you.

Luke 17 recounts the story of Jesus healing ten lepers, only one of whom came back and thanked Jesus for what He had done. It made quite an impression on Jesus.

> *One of them, when he saw he was healed, came back,*
> *praising God in a loud voice. He threw himself at Jesus'*
> *feet and thanked him—and he was a Samaritan.*
>
> *Jesus asked, "Were not all ten cleansed? Where are the*
> *other nine? Was no one found to return and give praise to*
> *God except this foreigner?" Then he said to him, "Rise*
> *and go; your faith has made you well." (verses 15-19)*

Other versions of Scripture translate the word *praise* as *glory*. In other words, thanking God for what He has done in our lives brings Him glory.

Offering thanks does two other things as well. First, it

builds our faith. As we recall God's goodness in the past, we can believe Him to move again. Because we remember God's faithfulness, we believe Him for the future. In his classic book *Prayer*, Ole Hallesby said, "If we have noted the Lord's answers to our prayers and thanked Him for what we have received of Him, then it becomes easier for us, and we get more courage, to pray for more."[5] Second, being thankful removes pride and replaces it with humility. Remember, "God opposes the proud but gives grace to the humble" (James 4:6; see also Proverbs 3:34).

So What?

As you begin to develop these two areas in your prayer life, you will see tremendous growth. Make every effort to include adoration and thanksgiving in your prayer time, even if it means ignoring intercession or petition for a time. Just as Jeremiah didn't mention his problems to God, praising God for who He is will have profound results in your own situations.

You may find it difficult to "adore" God at first. If that is the case, use Scripture to express your heart. Pray psalms (see chapter 10); go to some of the great passages in Paul's epistles (Romans 11:33-36; Philippians 2:5-11); praise God out of Revelation; use passages from Isaiah, such as chapter 53. Let God's Word give you the words of praise to declare back to Him!

Begin collecting lists of the scriptural names and phrases used to describe God, Jesus Christ, and the Holy Spirit. Then use that list to give you ways to praise Him. *Experiencing God* by Henry Blackaby and Claude King provides a nine-page list of the names, titles, and descriptions of God.[6] Put that list in your Bible and use it to foster adoration.

Use praise and worship tapes to stimulate worship and praise within you. Or, to help generate a heart of thanksgiving, keep a journal to record answers to prayer and revelations of what God has done for you. Thank Him for those. From time to time, recall them in prayer, just like Jeremiah did.

Adoration and thanksgiving are two powerful aspects to prayer. Don't neglect them!

For Further Reading

Experiencing God, Henry Blackaby and Claude V. King (Broadman & Holman)

A Love Affair with God, C. Welton Gaddy (Broadman & Holman)

The Heart of Praise, Jack Hayford (Regal)

The Art of Prayer, Timothy Jones (Ballantine Books)

Prayer Power Unlimited, J. Oswald Sanders (Discovery House)

__9

SPIRITUAL WARFARE PRAYER

THE INTENSITY OF OUR PRAYERS WAS RISING. OUR STAFF WAS LIFTING up a situation hindering *Pray!* magazine. We had been experiencing unusual problems with mailing it. Many subscribers were not getting their copies; others were receiving two copies. Research into the problem seemed to indicate that it was beyond simple human error. Something unusual was happening.

"And I say to you, Satan," declared one of our team, "that you have no authority to hinder *Pray!* and the mailing of it. You are to take your hands off. I declare this in the name of Jesus of Nazareth who came in the flesh! In the name of Jesus, I come against any curses that have been placed upon the magazine, and say they are broken."

Have you ever been in a prayer meeting or praying with someone when it sounded like someone was talking to Satan and not to God? *What was that?* you wondered. *Should I be doing that?*

That—and the example of my staff member—was a form of spiritual warfare. Sometimes during prayer, a person will be led to confront Satan or the demonic. Jesus Himself did this when he rebuked Peter: "'Get behind me, Satan!' he said. 'You do not have in mind the things of God, but the things of men'"

(Mark 8:33). At numerous times Jesus commanded a demon (or demons) to come out of an individual. And Jesus gave this authority to His followers: "When Jesus had called the Twelve together, he gave them power and authority to drive out all demons and to cure diseases" (Luke 9:1).

As His followers, we too have access to that power: "I have given you authority to trample on snakes and scorpions and to overcome all the power of the enemy; nothing will harm you. However, do not rejoice that the spirits submit to you, but rejoice that your names are written in heaven" (Luke 10:19-20). Some would believe that this power was only given to those to whom Jesus was speaking here (seventy-two followers He sent out in ministry). Yet we see Paul taking authority over demonic spirits (Acts 16:16-18), and he wasn't among the seventy-two. And Ephesians 6 gives us ample proof that we will regularly be involved in warfare, because we are told to put on armor for the battle.

There is no question that warfare is biblical, but is it something every believer should practice? Let me answer that in a roundabout way.

—— What Is Spiritual Warfare?

First of all, I believe all prayer that prays toward something, that asks for something to happen, that asks for God to move in a situation, is spiritual warfare. Remember an interaction between Jesus and Peter that occurred shortly before Jesus' arrest. "Simon, Simon," Jesus told Peter, "Satan has asked to sift you as wheat. But I have prayed for you, Simon, that your faith may not fail. And when you have turned back, strengthen your brothers" (Luke 22:31-32). Jesus didn't say that He came against Satan, rather that He prayed for Peter. That was warfare.

Likewise, when I pray for my daughter, Amy—that she

would become the woman of God that He intends her to be—that, too, is warfare. When I pray, asking God to develop my pastor into a man of prayer and of the Word, that, too, is warfare. Why are these examples warfare? Because if God answers these requests on behalf of my daughter and pastor, they are exactly opposite of what Satan wants to see happen. If these requests come true in their lives (and they will), then in a very real way Satan is defeated in their lives—at least in these areas.

Don't worry about confronting Satan directly (more on this later). Instead develop as a pray-er who storms the gates of heaven on behalf of yourself and others. Learn to pray kingdom prayers (see chapter 11) and you will be doing significant warfare. In fact, the most famous passage on warfare in the Bible, Ephesians 6:10-18, ends not by telling you to go out and attack Satan, but to "be alert and always keep on praying for all the saints."

—— No Need to Fear

Because to some extent all prayer is warfare, as you develop in your prayer life you will be growing in spiritual warfare as well. Spiritual warfare expert Tom White reminds us:

> Any saint who gets serious about prayer, worship, interceding for the lost, and bringing in an end-time harvest of souls is a target for enemy opposition and may begin to feel the pressure of this resistance in his or her own walk with God, home, and relationships. As this kind of saint, you become a kingdom "asset" that threatens Satan's status quo. The enemy has a file on you that circulates in the "situation room" of hell. Fortunately, God has a file on you, too. And it's tucked away in the courts of heaven.[1]

Should that scare you? No! God wants you to grow and He will give you all the warfare tools you need to withstand Satan. Jesus, in His Last Supper prayer, said, "My prayer is not that you [the Father] take them [believers] out of the world but that you protect them from the evil one" (John 17:15).

As you develop in this area of prayer, meditate on Psalm 91, which is full of encouragement and promise:

> *He who dwells in the shelter of the Most High*
> *will rest in the shadow of the Almighty.*
> *I will say of the LORD, "He is my refuge and my fortress,*
> *my God, in whom I trust." . . .*
> *If you make the Most High your dwelling—*
> *even the LORD, who is my refuge—*
> *then no harm will befall you,*
> *no disaster will come near your tent.*
> *For he will command his angels concerning you*
> *to guard you in all your ways. (verses 1-2,9-11)*

And Proverbs 14:26 reminds us, "He who fears the LORD has a secure fortress, and for his children it will be a refuge." Fearing God and taking refuge in Him are powerful warfare weapons.

Praise is another area of prayer that helps develop your warfare abilities. According to Psalm 22:3, God "inhabitest the praises of Israel [or, His people]" (KJV). Another way of putting it: God dwells in the praises of His people. While I don't know fully what that means, I do know that Satan hates it when we praise God (because he wants to be worshiped instead). Therefore, he runs from us when we praise God. How does praise work as a weapon?

Prayer leader Mell Winger offers five ways:

1. Praise honors the Father, first and foremost. In the Lord's Prayer, Jesus taught us to praise Him as a beginning point in prayer. Psalm 29:2 says we are to give Him the glory due His name. Praise builds faith by magnifying our perception of God's greatness.

2. Praise helps us know God better. It rehearses our knowledge of Him, and we come to know Him as what we praise Him to be. For example, if we praise Him as a mighty warrior, our understanding of His power grows. If we praise His names and titles, we gain perspective on His attributes.

3. God inhabits the praises of His people (Ps. 22:3). . . . Praise sensitizes us to His presence. When we know His nearness, we have courage for battle.

4. Praise breaks the enemy's opposition. A clear picture of this is found in Acts 16:25-26. When Paul and Silas praised God, all the prison doors were opened and everyone's chains came loose. Praise lifts us out of our own oppression (selfishness, heaviness, weariness, etc.), so we can better focus on the King of Glory and pray with faith.

5. Praise confuses the forces of darkness. Take a look at three Old Testament references to the power of praise in battle: 2 Chron. 20:21ff, Ps. 8:2, Ps. 145:5-9.

Praise poises us to battle from a position of victory instead of for victory. It is truly one of our most powerful spiritual weapons.[2]

Another area to develop is discernment of evil. We live in an era in which much of the moral blacks and whites have faded to gray. As believers, we allow incredible evil into our lives through what we watch on television and video, what we read, and so on. Because of this, we are very desensitized to evil's threat. Pray for the ability to discern. And when God speaks to you about something you shouldn't do because of its evil influence, pray for courage to obey.

White offers five steps to take when we discern evil in our battle:

1. Stand on and speak forth scriptural truth (2 Thess. 3:3, 1 Jn. 3:8, 1 Jn. 4:4).
2. Pray alertly "for the saints" (spouse, children, roommates, etc.) using the sword of the Spirit and the shield of faith to ward off enemy assaults (Eph. 6:16-18).
3. Apply the name and blood of Jesus to overcome enemy influence (Rev. 12:10-11).
4. Ask God to provide helping angels (Ps. 91, Heb. 1:4).
5. Discern and deal quickly with ungodly influences that threaten the home.[3]

If you develop these three areas (prayer, praise, and discernment) you'll be well on the way as a warfare pray-er. But should you ever pray like *Pray!*'s staff member, directly confronting Satan? Yes, there may very likely be occasions to do this. But when? And how?

First, I believe that direct confrontation with Satan will be very rare. In my own life, I would estimate that it occurs *a half of a percent* of the time. In other words, I almost always pray to God—even if I am "doing warfare." But at times I sense a clear burden from God to confront satanic forces. I don't do it simply "to cover my bases." Some people confront demonic forces to make sure they have covered every angle—just in case it might be an attack of the demonic. But not every evil or sinful situation is a *direct* result of the Evil One. Many things come as the result of our own flesh or of the godless world system around us. Ultimately, however, the fault belongs to Satan. Ephesians 6:12 reminds us that "our struggle is not against flesh and blood, but against the rulers, against the authorities, against the powers of this dark world and against the spiritual forces of evil in the heavenly realms."

You will at times be led to confront demonic forces. But primarily, you should do warfare by practicing these things:

1. Defensive prayer. Ask God for protection for you, your family, your pastor, your church.
2. Offensive prayer. Ask God to provide angels to come alongside a situation and war on your behalf.
3. Daily preparation. Put on the armor of God. (Ephesians 6:10-18)

So what should you do around others who practice this regularly? I would neither be critical nor feel the need to engage in this practice more. Rely on the Holy Spirit to guide you, not one man's or woman's prayer style. God will move some people to pray against Satan more often than others. Further explanation of this will come in chapter 12 "Finding Your Prayer Style." (To quickly explain: a person who has the spiritual gift of discernment or prophecy will likely practice confronting spirits more regularly than someone who has another spiritual gift.)

So What?

In closing, let me encourage you to do three things to grow in spiritual warfare praying.

First, simply develop your relationship with God. Get to know Him through prayer and reading His Word. As your relationship with Him grows, you will naturally pray more and more about what's on God's heart—that's warfare.

Second, develop an attitude of humility. Some people become cocky when engaging in direct spiritual warfare. Perhaps this is because they recognize our authority in Christ, which is biblically true. But that attitude can quickly turn into pride. First Peter 5:6-10 cautions:

> *Humble yourselves, therefore, under God's mighty hand, that he may lift you up in due time. Cast all your anxiety on him because he cares for you.*
> *Be self-controlled and alert. Your enemy the devil prowls around like a roaring lion looking for someone to devour. Resist him, standing firm in the faith. . . . And the God of all grace, who called you to his eternal glory in Christ, after you have suffered a little while, will himself restore you and make you strong, firm and steadfast.*

In other words, we have more strength to resist Satan when we are humble. We stand more firmly when we recognize that we need God's help to do so.

Third, read, meditate upon, and even memorize these two warfare passages of Scripture: Psalm 91 and Ephesians 6:10-18. Then let God guide you deeper into this area.

For Further Reading

Binding and Loosing, K. Neil Foster and Paul King (Christian Publications)

The Authority of the Believer, J. A. MacMillan (Christian Publications)

"War: Standing Against the Forces of Darkness," (*Pray!* Issue 5, March/April 1998)

The Believer's Guide to Spiritual Warfare, Tom White (Servant)

Breaking Strongholds: How Spiritual Warfare Sets Captives Free, Tom White (Servant)

Section 3

More EFFECTIVE
PRAYER

─ 10

PRAYING SCRIPTURE

THE YEAR WAS 1993. I WAS IN CEDAR RAPIDS, IOWA, REPRESENTing my employer at a pastor's conference. I had only recently finished reading Richard Foster's new book, *Prayer.* For the previous four years, God had been taking me on an incredible journey into prayer.

My journey had really begun when I arrived at Christian Publications and my first assignment was to write a study guide to A. W. Tozer's classic best-seller *The Pursuit of God.* Over the course of a year I had read that book a dozen times. No one can read it without hungering for more of God. I was no different.

Over the next three years, I read numerous books on prayer—even taught a thirteen-week adult Sunday school class on the topic several times.

Now, here I was listening to Dr. Joe Arthur, a pastor and former missionary, talk about his own journey into prayer. It was filled with exciting stories—a phenomenal healing, amazing numbers of people coming to Christ, and so on. But the most intriguing thing to me was his description of a simple prayer practice that in all my journey and reading I had never heard before—the power of praying Scripture. It seemed so basic, yet

I had never considered it. Oh, I had heard people use a phrase like, "Lord, You've said in Your Word … ," then quote part of a verse. But I never realized what a tool that could be.

In one session, Dr. Arthur even had us practice the technique with a partner. Using Psalm 71, we were instructed to go back and forth, verse by verse, praying the psalm. We could use phrases from the verse and add to them, or simply pray the verse almost word for word. It was wonderful.

That simple lesson opened up a whole new world for me. But why? What makes praying Scripture so powerful—revolutionary even?

—— WHY PRAY SCRIPTURE?

"When I turn what Scripture says about God into meditation, prayer, and praise," said Jane McClain, "I relate to Him more intimately, praise Him more effectively, soak up His love more fully, and pray His will more soundly."[1] It can really do all that? Yes!

Prayer naturally brings us to the Word, and God's Word should always bring us to prayer. The two go together. Unfortunately, most of us keep them separated at all times. We have our time to read the Bible and our time to pray. It was revolutionary to me when I learned to put them together. I could start to read a chapter in the Bible, but flow in and out of prayer as I did. That practice made God's Word stand out more as I meditated and asked Him questions about it.

Previously, I had from time to time experienced the voice of the Holy Spirit illuminating a verse or phrase or passage to my heart. And occasionally I had felt the exhilaration that comes from knowing God had shed personal light through His Word. But with this new practice, I experienced that phenomenon on a very regular basis. Scripture reading came more alive for me and I wanted to do it more, which in turn produced a more meaningful prayer life.

Praying God's Word gives us a deeper sense of what to pray for a situation. I don't know about you, but I often struggle to find the words to pray. I mean, I can pray the obvious for a situation. My friend Joe needs a new job; I pray that he'll get one. I tried to regularly pray for my daughter, Amy, but nothing more than the everyday stuff came to mind: that she'd do well in school, grow in her faith, be protected from evil influences, that sort of thing. Scripture gives me a better idea of meaningful things to pray. Now I keep a list of thirty-one biblical virtues from a *Pray!* article by Bob Hostetler in my Bible. Each one is based upon the language of a verse. For example, for Amy I may pray number five, "Self-control," which is based on 1 Thessalonians 5:6: "Father, help Amy not to be like many others around her, but let her be alert and self-controlled in all she does."[2]

McClain concurs with this principle. She tells of a time when a friend called asking her to pray for his brother, Jerry, a pastor, who had just had a heart attack. Jane wanted to pray for more than just Jerry's healing and comfort for the family. So she turned to Psalm 138:

> The first verses praise God, which is always an appropriate place to start. The third verse says, "When I called, you answered me; you made me bold." So I boldly asked that God answer quickly. The next verses tell about kings giving thanks to God because of David's testimony. Since Jerry was a pastor, I prayed these verses, assuming that more people needed to hear his messages and turn to the Lord.
>
> Verse seven says, "Though I walk in the midst of trouble, you preserve my life." I prayed that God would revive Jerry. The psalm ends, "The LORD will fulfill his purpose for me; your love, O LORD, endures forever — do not abandon the

works of your hands." I prayed believing God would not forsake Jerry. I closed my Bible, feeling assured that I'd done my part and that God would do His. A few days later, Charlie told me that his brother had gone home from the hospital and was doing much better.[3]

Finally, praying Scripture is powerful because we are confident that we are praying God's will for a situation. First John 5:14-15 says, "This is the confidence we have in approaching God: that if we ask anything according to his will, he hears us. And if we know that he hears us—whatever we ask—we know that we have what we asked of him."

If I am praying for my friend Joe's job situation, I may not know if the job he is being interviewed for is God's will for him. But I do know that it is God's will that Joe may be counted worthy of His calling and that by God's power working in him, he might fulfill every good purpose God has called him to (2 Thessalonians 1:11). I do know that God has a perfect plan for Joe, plans to prosper him and not harm him, to give him hope and a future (Jeremiah 29:11). I can pray those things for Joe and be fully confident that they will come to pass.

—— WHEN TO PRAY SCRIPTURE

There are a number of ways you can incorporate Scripture in your prayers:

Devotional time. As you are reading the Bible, if something surprises or delights you, express that emotion in a quick prayer of praise to God. For example, I might read Romans 7:21–8:2. When I come to the verse "Therefore, there is now no condemnation for those who are in Christ Jesus, because through Christ Jesus the law of the Spirit of life set me free from the law of sin and death" (8:1-2), I might pray, "Father, I thank

You that because of Christ, I am no longer condemned. Thank You for the gift of Your Son. Thank You that I am free from sin and death."

If the Word offers something you desire, pause in your reading and offer that desire in a prayer to God. For example, I read the phrase in Romans 8:6, "but the mind controlled by the Spirit is life and peace." I pray, "Holy Spirit, I desire a mind of life and peace, a mind controlled by You. Please take control of my mind. Show me those hidden places not yet controlled by You."

The prompting of the Holy Spirit. While praying, sometimes a passage or verse of Scripture will come to mind. The Holy Spirit is probably prompting you to pray that Scripture over the situation. I find that sometimes when I am praying, the Holy Spirit will direct me to randomly thumb through my Bible. I often land on a verse that seems perfect to pray for a situation.

Deliberately praying Scripture. Great for group prayer, this method instructs participants to select a *specific* passage to pray over a situation—like Jane McClain did for Jerry. At the last corporate prayer meeting of the year, my church was focusing on the vision and plans for the next year. I had everyone turn to Ephesians and instructed them to pray only thoughts and phrases based on its verses. To me, it was one of the most powerful prayer meetings we had ever had. Why? Because it was rich with God's Word, and because of that, it focused on His will for us.

—— HOW TO PRAY SCRIPTURE

There are no right or wrong ways to use Scripture in your prayers. But here are a few easy methods to keep in mind.

Reminding God. One way is simply to remind God what He said. Using 2 Corinthians 10:5, you might pray,

Lord, you have said in Your Word, that "we demolish arguments and every pretension that sets itself up against the knowledge of God, and we take captive every thought to make it obedient to Christ." Right now we claim that promise. In the name of Jesus, we demolish the stronghold in Mary's life right now. We say that no longer will she hold to her wrong thinking about leaving her husband. We demolish her self-absorbed arguments in Jesus' name.

Adapt-a-verse. The most common form of praying Scripture, adapt-a-verse simply means to incorporate scriptural thoughts and phrases into your prayer. "Father, fill Susan with Your Spirit. Cause her to bear fruit in every good work as she grows in the knowledge of You. Strengthen her so she might have endurance and patience for what's ahead in her ministry" (Colossians 1:9-11).

Proclaim God's Word. Pastors do this often when they close a service. Many use a verse like Jude 24-25 and proclaim it as true over a congregation: "To him who is able to keep you from falling and to present you before his glorious presence without fault and with great joy—to the only God our Savior, be glory, majesty, power and authority, through Jesus Christ our Lord, before all ages, now and forevermore! Amen."

Find a promise. Another excellent method is to seek God for a promise in a given situation. Many believers have done this over the years. Dawson Trotman, the founder of The Navigators, was a master at claiming promises. As he wrestled in prayer over what God might be telling him to do, he would look for a specific verse to pray. He would "claim" it as God's truth in the situation.

When I was going through the breakup of my marriage, I often spent the weekends at my parents' cottage at Delta Lake Bible Conference Center in Rome, New York. One weekend, a friend put a Bible verse on a piece of paper and stuck it under my windshield wiper. It was Jeremiah 29:11: "'For I know the plans I have for you' declares the LORD, 'plans to prosper you and not to harm you, plans to give you hope and a future.'" I claimed that promise in prayer over and over and over. Today God has blessed me with a wonderful wife and daughter, a fantastic job where I can serve Him, and a house big enough to provide a home for my parents. I almost couldn't ask for any more—except now I am claiming Jabez's prayer as my promise (see chapters 5 and 14).

So What?

I promise that praying Scripture will be one of the most profound tools you can add to your prayer life. It will enrich you. It will deepen your walk with God like no other kind of praying can. And you will experience His power on a regular basis as you see prayers answered that you knew were His will for your life.

Try it.

For Further Reading

Praying Scripture, Judson Cornwell (Creation House)
Praying God's Word, Beth Moore (Broadman & Holman)
All the Prayers of the Bible, Herbert Lockyer (Zondervan)
Listening to God, Jan Johnson (NavPress)

— 11

KINGDOM–FOCUSED PRAYER

"PLEASE PRAY FOR MY AUNT MARTHA," COMES A PLEA FROM THE back of the room. "She hurt her foot and is having trouble walking."

"And don't forget Susan's daughter, Wendy, at CU," pipes up another. "Susan said she was having trouble in her biology class and a major test was coming up this week."

"Pray for Bill. He's having a dispute with his neighbor. Pray that his neighbor will see Bill's point of view and give in."

You've heard such requests before because they're typical of most prayer groups or church prayer meetings. Sometimes a request stirs up emotion in you or one of the other pray-ers, and you're able to pray with passion, but usually you pray out of duty to the one requesting prayer. No thought is given as to what to pray—what God wants to do in the situation. The prayer is for the obvious—that Aunt Martha's foot would get better, that Wendy would remember what she studied and pass the test, that Bill's neighbor would calm down and give in to Bill's opinion.

While nothing is wrong with people asking for prayer for these types of problems or situations, and nothing is wrong with praying for them either, still there is something unexciting about them. Unless people are directly involved in the problem or related to those who are, most find it hard to drum up much enthusiasm for such prayers. The reason? These are not needs that easily generate kingdom-focused prayers.

As you grow in your prayer life, if you haven't already found this to be true, you will: Intercession will often become boring. When that happens, people begin to respond in one of two ways when asked to pray for a need: They agree to pray, but quickly forget about it, or they pray only out of guilt or obligation. Either response is not a good solution.

Again, the answer lies in learning to pray kingdom-focused prayers. What do I mean by kingdom-focused prayer? Simply this: When we pray for something that has lasting value and importance in the kingdom of God, or when we can turn our prayers for a situation into prayers about kingdom issues (ones that we know are releasing God's will—remember chapter 1), then we are praying kingdom-focused prayers.

Remember the Holy Spirit's role in prayer? When "we do not know what we ought to pray for, . . . the Spirit intercedes for us" (Romans 8:26). Kingdom-focused prayers are ones that are more fully in line with what we "ought to pray for," with what the Holy Spirit is interceding in the situation.

—— THE MODEL OF PAUL

So how do our prayers become kingdom-focused? The apostle Paul provides a model for us.

Paul certainly had a lot of people under his care. People with needs, people who faced life-and-death situations. Yet in all of his New Testament letters, I can't find any evidence that Paul prayed for an obvious, logical answer to a specific need. The only time I see him mentioning something "need-oriented" is in 2 Corinthians 12, where he prayed that his "thorn in the flesh"—something that was tormenting him—would be removed. God refused his request three times.

Let's look at what he prayed for these people who had such tremendous needs.

The church in Rome. "May the God who gives endurance and encouragement give you a spirit of unity among yourselves as you follow Christ Jesus, so that with one heart and mouth you may glorify the God and Father of our Lord Jesus Christ" (Romans 15:5-6). "May the God of hope fill you with all joy and peace as you trust in him, so that you may overflow with hope by the power of the Holy Spirit" (verse 13).

Even though the church was probably experiencing persecution, and these believers were just trying to survive in a city hostile to Christianity, Paul didn't pray for protection or safety. (If it were me, I know those things would be at the top of my prayer list!) Rather, Paul prayed for unity, joy, and peace. Why? Both verses give us a "so that." Unity of believers would bring glory to God. Jesus prayed for unity of believers in John 17:20-21: "My prayer is . . . that all of them may be one, Father, . . . so that the world may believe that you have sent me."

Jesus also said, "But I, when I am lifted up from the earth, will draw all men to myself" (John 12:32). Paul knew that when outsiders saw the unity of the church, they would be drawn to Jesus Christ in great numbers. Therefore, rather than pray for the obvious—protection—he prayed with kingdom eyes, pleading for unity so people would be attracted to Christ. Paul also prayed for the Roman Christians to experience joy and peace amid the turmoil of their lives. Why? So that they would overflow with hope. People who have hope in tough times are also attractive to those who don't have hope. People without hope will want what believers have. Again, Paul knew that people would come to Christ if they saw hope in believers. In other words, he saw with kingdom eyes ("Lord, give them hope") rather than earthly eyes ("Lord, get them out of this").

The church in Ephesus. The Ephesian believers were also under intense pressure and persecution. Ephesus was the center of the worship of the goddess Diana (Acts 19). Paul had almost been killed by an angry mob on one of his visits there, so he knew the stress and pressure the believers there were under. But again, rather than pray the obvious for them, he prayed for their spiritual development.

> *Ever since I heard about your faith in the Lord Jesus and your love for all the saints, I have not stopped giving thanks for you, remembering you in my prayers. I keep asking that the God of our Lord Jesus Christ, the glorious Father, may give you the Spirit of wisdom and revelation, so that you may know him better. I pray also that the eyes of your heart may be enlightened in order that you may know the hope to which he has called you, the riches of his glorious inheritance in the saints, and his incomparably great power for us who believe. (Ephesians 1:15-19)*

Later Paul prayed,

> *... that out of [God's] glorious riches he may strengthen you with power through his Spirit in your inner being, so that Christ may dwell in your hearts through faith. And I pray that you, being rooted and established in love, may have power, together with all the saints, to grasp how wide and long and high and deep is the love of Christ, and to know this love that surpasses knowledge—that you may be filled to the measure of all the fullness of God. (3:16-19)*

I don't know about you, but if I had a sore foot, I think I'd be more excited by someone praying that I might "be filled to the measure of all the fullness of God" than someone praying "Lord, heal his foot." That's kingdom-focused prayer.

And the pattern continues in the rest of Paul's prayers.

The church in Philippi. "And this is my prayer: *that your love may abound more and more in knowledge and depth of insight, so that* you may be able to discern what is best and may be pure and blameless until the day of Christ, filled with the fruit of righteousness that comes through Jesus Christ—to the glory and praise of God" (Philippians 1:9-11, emphasis added).

The church of Colosse. "For this reason, since the day we heard about you, we have not stopped praying for you and asking God to *fill you with the knowledge of his will through all spiritual wisdom and understanding.* And we pray this in order that you may live a life worthy of the Lord and may please him in every way: bearing fruit in every good work, growing in the knowledge of God, being strengthened with all power according to his glorious might so that you may have great endurance and patience" (Colossians 1:9-11, emphasis added).

The church at Thessalonica. "May the Lord *make your love increase and overflow for each other and for everyone else,* just as ours does for you. May *he strengthen your hearts* so that you will be blameless and holy in the presence of our God and Father when our Lord Jesus comes with all his holy ones" (1 Thessalonians 3:12-13, emphasis added). "May God himself, the God of peace, *sanctify you through and through. May your whole spirit, soul and body be kept blameless at the coming of our Lord Jesus Christ*" (5:23, emphasis added). "May our Lord Jesus Christ himself and God our Father, who loved us and by his grace gave us eternal encouragement and good hope, *encourage your hearts and strengthen you in every good deed and word*" (2 Thessalonians 2:16-17, emphasis added).

Prayer for Philemon. "I pray that *you may be active in sharing your faith,* so that you will have a full understanding of every good thing we have in Christ" (verse 6, emphasis added).

Notice that in his prayers, Paul seemed to pray for the process, not the results. That is an interesting distinction. But also notice that in most of these prayers, Paul did have some thought of intended results; there is just no indication that he prayed for the results.

Look back at his prayer for the Philippians. He wanted them to discern what was best, to be pure and blameless. But he didn't pray for that; he prayed that their love would abound more and more, especially in their knowledge and insight of the depths of Christ's love.

So What?

So what does this mean for you as you pray?

Don't be quick to pray for the obvious desired results in a situation. Consider the situation. Try to think of some kingdom-impacting things you could pray for. Pray for spiritual growth in the lives of those involved in the situation. Pray for fruit of the Spirit to be developed in their lives. Pray for Christlikeness and character. Ask God how you should pray. If nothing comes to you, perhaps pray Scripture.

When my daughter, Amy, was in sixth grade—her first year of middle school—she struggled. A giving, sensitive girl, Amy soon began to get picked on, not only by her classmates, but by her friends as well. As a father, I wanted a quick solution to the problem.

First, I simply downplayed things. "Middle school kids are mean, Amy," I would say. "Just don't let it bother you." But it started getting her down. Her grades were suffering. She was starting to dislike school—a first for her.

I can't honestly say I never prayed for the obvious results—

that kids would stop picking on her, that her work habits would improve, that she would like school again. But for the most part I focused my prayers for her elsewhere. I prayed that Christlikeness would be developed in her, that her faith in Christ would become more vibrant and real. And God worked.

But how He answered was very unexpected. Amy's prayer life grew by leaps and bounds as she poured out her heart to Jesus. And the biggest answer came in a change God made in my wife and me.

God led us to do something we never thought of doing— homeschooling Amy in seventh grade. While it has not been easy, it has been a blessing. We have gained insights into Amy we never had before, and those insights have fueled our prayers for her. We have watched her grow spiritually through serious Bible study and a more active devotional life.

I never would have thought to pray about the possibility of homeschooling Amy. Yet clearly, this was God's will for us. As we prayed for kingdom values to be birthed in her, this was where God led us.

In its simplest form, that is kingdom-focused praying. Pray for biblical virtues and character, and leave the results to God. While it is not wrong to pray for specific results, when we primarily pray for spiritual growth and for God to be glorified, amazing things will happen.

For Further Reading

A Time to Pray God's Way, Evelyn Christenson (Harvest House)
What God Does When Women Pray, Evelyn Christenson (Word)
Beyond Imagination, Dick Eastman (Chosen Books)
The Jericho Hour, Dick Eastman (Creation House)
Prayer That Shapes the Future, Brad Long and Doug McMurry
    (Zondervan)

— 12

FINDING YOUR PRAYER STYLE

M Y MIND KEPT WANDERING. I WASN'T GOING TO MAKE IT through this prayer meeting. Prayer after lengthy prayer covered everything mentioned during request time. On my knees, with my head in my arms, I was fighting sleep. I only held passionate interest in two or three of the issues being prayed about. Was I just a sluggard? A weak Christian, bored with the goings-on?

No. I had run smack dab into the middle of a prayer meeting filled with "list pray-ers" and people with the gift of mercy.

For many of us, growth in our prayer lives comes slowly because we never learn a basic truth about prayer. Just as our individual personalities differ, so should our prayer styles differ. Just as our spiritual gifts differ, so will those different gifts affect the way we pray. There is no "one size fits all" style when it comes to prayer.

Some people are very emotional when they pray. They seem to pour their hearts into the issue at hand. They pray passionately, often with tears or with great dramatics in their voice. But is that the model for all of us? Do we know we've arrived when we can pray like that?

Others need to have a list in front of them. They make sure they cover everything. When they pray in a group, if it appears someone's request was missed, they'll jump back in and remember it. Still other individuals pray almost militantly, seeming to rebuke Satan and demons almost as much as they address God.

Some believers pray almost exclusively using Scripture. They base their prayers on the Psalms or on the Lord's Prayer. Others carry on a two-way conversation, saying something, then waiting for an answer, talking, listening, talking, listening. Some can only pray short thoughts; others pray for minutes—even hours—on end. Many believers often pray using a spiritual language or "tongues." They often don't even understand exactly what they are praying.

And different cultures often pray in different ways. Some ethnic believers, when in a group prayer meeting, all pray at one time. Many Korean and African-American churches pray this way.

I recall the struggle one of our designers had with our staff prayer times at NavPress. She had come to Christ through the ministry of the Brooklyn Tabernacle, a church where everyone raises their voices in prayer at the same time. We staid, Caucasian evangelicals were only used to praying one at a time. She tried to change us, but to no avail. Two styles had collided.

One time when I was in a prayer meeting with members of America's National Prayer Committee, I experienced a style I had never heard before. I was praying in a group that included a Hispanic brother, Ephraim. When Ephraim started to pray, it became a combination of spoken words and sentences, grunts and groans, and even sung phrases. It was one of the most beautiful styles I had ever heard.

But is one of these styles the correct one? Should we force ourselves into it? No! As you grow in prayer, you need to find your prayer style and then primarily develop that style. Does that mean you should never pray another way or that you should refuse to pray with people who pray in another style? Certainly not. Learning to appreciate prayer diversity is beneficial both to us individually and to the unity of the church. We all need to continually fight being in a box or a rut in regard to prayer. I always recommend that believers try new things with prayer—new methods, new subjects, new locations. Anything that can keep prayer fresh and invigorating.

So how do we find our style?

‒‒ PRAYER AND SPIRITUAL GIFTS

We start by finding our spiritual gift. When we accept Christ as our Savior and the Holy Spirit indwells us, He gives each of us a special gift to serve the church (see Romans 12 and 1 Corinthians 12). Recognizing our spiritual gift is important because many spiritual gifts affect the way we pray.

Prayer leader Alice Smith is a pioneer in the relationship between spiritual gifts and prayer styles. She and her husband, Eddie, have spent years researching and studying intercessors and prayer styles. Smith writes,

> According to 1 Corinthians 12, "There are different kinds of gifts" (v. 4), "different kinds of service" (v. 5), and "different kinds of working" (v. 6). Intercessors who possess different spiritual gifts (such as mercy, teaching, or word of knowledge) will pray differently. And God's discipline in each life will affect each person's depth in prayer. Just as we need diversity of gifts in the body, different kinds of intercessors are required to complete the whole ministry of intercession. If we can understand and put these differences to work, God will be blessed, the enemy crippled, and [our church] united in powerful prayer.[1]

But how does this relationship between spiritual gifts and prayer styles work? Smith lists nine different kinds of intercessors in her analysis:

- Flexible Intercessors. These intercessors do not adhere to any method or style. They are pliable in God's hand, discern the Spirit's direction, and can adapt to any style.
- Crisis Intercessors. These intercessors get into praying for others who are experiencing crisis. They sense the urgency and can easily go to prayer.
- Intercessors for the Nations. These intercessors find it easy to pray for the lost around the world.
- Mercy-Motivated Intercessors. Because of their merciful hearts, these intercessors find great satisfaction in praying for any person or situation needing divine mercy.
- Prayer-List Intercessors. These intercessors are perseverers. When God burdens them to pray for someone or something, it goes on their prayer list and is not forgotten.
- Prophetic Intercessors. These intercessors hear from God regularly. They often pray with great vision when lifting up situations.
- Special Assignment Intercessors. These people feel called or "assigned" to lift up specific religious, political, or social leaders regularly in prayer. God may give them a great burden to regularly pray for the President, for example.
- Warfare Intercessors. These intercessors seem to be able to scan the heavenlies for signs of trouble. When God reveals enemy targets or strongholds, these people can do battle in prayer.
- Administrative Intercessors. These intercessors may have differing prayer styles. They are great organizers and encouragers to see that things are prayed for.[2]

Perhaps you see yourself in one of these descriptions; perhaps you are just trying to understand where you might fit. Well, if you know your spiritual gift, here's where you might fit:

Do you have a gift of mercy? You might pray with a crisis or mercy-motivated style. Do you have the gift of faith? Perhaps you fit best in the warfare, prophetic, nations, or crisis categories. Pastoral gifts? Perhaps you pray best as a special assignment or crisis, mercy-motivated intercessor. Do you have the gift of administration? Then administrative or prayer-list might be your primary style. Gift of evangelism? Intercessing for the nations might be your thing. For a more complete list, read Smith's article at *www.praymag.com* (click on "Search the Archives" and type "Alice Smith" in the search engine).

While none of these are cut and dried, a knowledge of where you might primarily fit can help you understand why you are most comfortable praying as you do.

—— PRAYER AND PERSONALITIES

The next step in discovering your prayer style is to see where your personality fits in. Optimists pray differently from pessimists. Intuitive people pray differently from concrete thinkers. Active people usually pray differently from less active ones. And all of this is okay. God has designed us to be that way.

Ask yourself these questions: (1) What personality traits shape me as a pray-er? (2) How can I use these traits to become a better pray-er?

Are you an active person who has trouble sitting down for fifteen minutes to pray? While praying for a length of time is always a good goal to shoot for, don't punish yourself if you can't—and don't force yourself into that box just to be disciplined if you don't get enjoyment from it. Try praying a number of shorter times throughout the day. Discipline yourself to pray, but don't feel you have to do fifteen minutes first thing in the morning. Perhaps look for different places to pray. If you exercise by walking or being on a piece of exercise equipment, pray while doing that.

If I were growing up nowadays, I would probably have been diagnosed as having Attention Deficit Disorder. I am easily distracted. As I attempted to pray for longer periods, I would constantly feel guilty because my mind got off track. I tried finding a place to pray where there would be no interruptions. But to no avail. Then I realized I can still be an effective prayer warrior without forcing it to happened at 6:30 in the morning. Rather than force myself into a style I couldn't sustain or enjoy, I looked for ways to improve my prayer life outside that box.

Because I was easily distracted, I thought, *Where's a place I can pray where I can get distracted without feeling guilt over it, and still get back on task?* Driving. I have a thirty-minute commute to work each day. I spend a lot of that time praying. Yes, my mind has to wander to the road. But I can immediately get back on task without chiding myself.

If you find a solution that fits your personality, develop it. Mark Phillips, a pastor from Amarillo, Texas, took praying while driving to another level. He dubbed his thirty-year-old pickup his "Mobile Prayer Closet." He puts on worship CDs to stimulate praying. He has a notepad stuck to his windshield with suction cups. On it he can write requests or Scripture verses he wants to memorize or pray through. He keeps a Bible handy for when he is stuck in traffic. He has learned to establish visual markers along his route that remind him to pray for a certain person or thing. And recognizing what a holy place his pickup could be, he anointed it with oil as an act of worship.[3] Recognizing the long drive he had five or six times a week and seeing it as "lost time," Mark redeemed it by turning a pickup truck into God's dwelling place.

So What?

Because you desire to grow in prayer, the most important point I can make in this chapter is, don't force yourself into someone else's prayer modes—or force them into yours.

When I was managing editor of *Discipleship Journal,* we received an article on praying the Psalms. It was a very good article, except that the author wanted to force people to do what he had found meaningful. He started the piece by attacking the prayer acronym ACTS (Adoration, Confession, Thanksgiving, Supplication), commenting that anyone who used that format was immature. What this author failed to understand was that even though his personality would never fit comfortably into the rigid mold ACTS required, the method did fit the styles and personalities of others. It didn't make them immature pray-ers, just different.

Understanding prayer styles and personalities is particularly important when you are praying in a group. If you are a short-prayer person, don't be intimidated by people who pray longer prayers. Fight against being annoyed by an emotional pray-er if you aren't one. Be yourself, and respect how others pray.

As you develop your style, try to discover the connection between your prayer style and your spiritual gift. If you find you have a gift of mercy, make sure you are feeding your prayer life with mercy-related intercession. If you have a gift of evangelism, make sure your prayers are loaded with requests for lost people you know. If you have a gift of administration, offer your services to your church to help oversee prayer ministries.

Because one of my spiritual gifts is faith, I am much more "jazzed" about praying for needs that require the miraculous. I also have a teaching gift. This combination makes me want to teach and encourage others about trusting God for the miraculous. So, without trying to push an agenda, I regularly try to challenge our church elders and board to risk, not to make a decision based solely on whether or not we *can* do something. I pray prayers that ask for God to move in mighty ways within our congregation. My church needs me. But it also needs my friend Marv (who by the way I love praying with). Marv sees the problem or the need clearly. Unlike me, who might soar off in a prayer that calls down miraculous workings of God, Marv prays with honest, matter-of-fact, sincere, impassioned pleas that rest in God's sovereignty. My church also needs Chuck. Among Chuck's spiritual gifts are discernment and tongues. Not surprisingly, he is a strong spiritual warfare pray-er. When we are praying for someone who needs physical or emotional healing, or is under bondage to something, Chuck's prayer style is vital.

Don't ever forget that your family and your church—and God—need you as a pray-er. Don't sit back and be annoyed in church prayer settings, and don't neglect your prayer life because you are trying to fit into someone else's box and can't. Start developing your individual style.

For Further Reading

Rees Howells: Intercessor, Norman Grubbs (Christian Literature Crusade)
Beyond the Veil, Alice Smith (Regal)
The Intercessory Prayer of Jesus, Warren Wiersbe (Baker)

__ 13

PRAYER AND GOD'S WILL

WHEN I WAS IN ELEMENTARY SCHOOL, MY DAD PASTORED Parkside Alliance Church, a small congregation in Watertown, New York. When we first moved there, the church had rented a nice apartment for my family. But the church also had an apartment (not as nice) above it. Because the church was struggling to meet financial obligations, my parents offered to move into the not-so-nice apartment, if the church would start to look for a permanent parsonage.

As the year and many prayers went by, the church wasn't improving financially, but an opportunity came its way. There was a large, somewhat rundown house next door to the church, the home of a couple of eccentric brothers who never threw anything out. The brothers died and the city put up the house for auction, selling it on the basis of sealed bids. The church bid $6,001 for a house that was worth far more than that. They got it!

But where would the money for remodeling come from? Church people started doing most of the work. As Christmas 1967 neared, a bill of nine hundred dollars was looming (a big sum of money in that day), with little money in the checkbook. The church continued to pray, and the board decided to take a special year-end offering for this need.

The church's annual membership meeting also came. Because things were tight, my parents were not expecting or wishing for a raise. Yet the congregation voted to give them one as a step of faith. And when the year-end offering was counted, more than nine hundred dollars was collected—plus a note from a nonmember who promised to pay for all the remodeling expenses (a gift of eventually more than $10,000).

Why did God choose to answer these people's prayers in such a dramatic, miraculous way? Because they were praying on the basis of the principle of 1 John 5:14-15: "This is the confidence we have in approaching God: *that if we ask anything according to his will,* he hears us. And if we know that he hears us—whatever we ask—we know that we have what we asked of him" (emphasis added). This passage is one of the most wonderful promises in the Bible. Yet it comes with a very important catch—what we ask *according to His will* will be answered.

—— How to Know God's Will

Hundreds of books have been written on how to know God's will, so a short chapter in a book on prayer cannot do justice to the subject. But there are some powerful insights I can offer on how to make sure you are praying "according to God's will" in a given situation.

Lee Brase, prayer director of The Navigators, has years of insight into prayer. Frequently, says Lee, our prayers are "preprayer," especially in group settings. When we pray alone, it is not uncommon to talk very honestly with God about a subject. (For me, phrases such as "Lord, I don't know what to pray in this situation," fall from my lips more when I am alone than when I pray in groups.) But when we participate in group prayer, we usually do one of two things. We either pray the obvious—exactly what the requester wants us to pray for (healing, a job, whatever). Or we corporately make sure all the bases are covered. In the case of an illness, someone prays for healing, another prays for strength to endure the illness (just in case God doesn't heal), another prays that God would receive glory in the situation. "Often we believe that our list of possibilities gives God a safety net," says my assistant, Sandie. "If He doesn't accomplish something one way, we give our permission for Him to do it in another way that makes sense to us."[1] The hope is that God's will in the situation is covered, and an answer will come.

Our prayers do not have to be like that. I firmly believe that in any situation God will reveal His will so we can focus on praying it, or there are things we know are His will that we can pray. So how do we pray His will?

Get right with God. The first step to discerning God's will in prayer is to make sure your heart is pure before Him. Has anything come between you and God to block the line of communication? (See chapter 15 for more explanation.) God will not reveal His will and purposes to people who are not living godly lives.

Ask the Holy Spirit. The next step in seeking God's will is simple: ask. If, as the Lord's Prayer states, we are to pray: "your will be done on earth as it is in heaven," (Matthew 6:10), then wouldn't it stand to reason that He should often reveal what it is so we can pray it? Earlier in the Matthew account, when speaking on how we should pray, Jesus said, "Do not keep on babbling like pagans, for they think they will be heard because of their many words" (verse 7). The King James Version calls babbling, "vain repetitions." Surely, Jesus would not want us to simply say over and over, "Your will be done, Your will be done," in our prayers—or just tack it on the end of a prayer as a "catch-all."

I believe that in many cases the Holy Spirit will reveal how we should pray. But this likely could take some time. In a fast-paced society that demands "fast everything," waiting to discern God's will is difficult. Too often we pray the first thing that pops into our head for a situation—and that's wrong. We need to seek God for what *He* wants to do in that situation. As you seek, begin to take note of what you become burdened to pray about. And don't worry if it seems a little unusual. Remember, even if you aren't right on target, the Holy Spirit is interceding on your behalf.

Read His Word. Spend extra time in Scripture as you pray. Look for a verse to claim, or pay attention to a passage that God seems to want you to meditate on. Listen for His voice. Start praying Scriptures over the situation. Look for verses that seem to pop out at you. Remember, the truth of Scripture is God's will. You can never go wrong praying scriptural truth over a situation.

George Mueller, a famous nineteenth-century Christian who ran orphanages in England, was well known for his faith in God to provide. Story after story is told of times when an orphanage was out of food, Mueller prayed, and the next morning food would be on the doorstep. Mueller was a mighty man of prayer. He had a six-step plan for seeking God's will.

1. I seek at the beginning to get my heart into such a state that it has no will of its own in regard to the given matter.
2. Having done this, I do not leave the result to feeling or simple impression. If I do so, I make myself liable to great delusions.
3. I seek the will of the Spirit through, or in connection with, the Word of God.
4. Next, I take into account providential circumstances. These often plainly indicate God's will in connection with His Word and Spirit.

5. 1 ask God in prayer to reveal His will to me aright.
6. Thus, through prayer to God, the study of the Word, and reflection, 1 come to a deliberate judgment according to the best of my ability and knowledge.[2]

So What?

"True prayer," said J. Oswald Sanders, "is not asking God for what we want but for what He wants. . . . Prayer is not a convenient method of getting one's own way or of bending God to one's desires. Prayer is the means by which our desires can be redirected and aligned with the will of God."[3] That's what happened with Jesus in the Garden of Gethsemane on the night of His arrest. While He struggled, His heart came into alignment with God's will. As you grow in your ability to pray God's will, that same sense of relinquishment—giving up your will and desires—will become easier.

As you begin your journey into seeking to always pray His will, let me leave you with four tips:

1. Determine not to pray the first thing that comes to mind—the obvious—over a situation. That may be what you are eventually led to pray, but fight the tendency to automatically go there first.
2. Seek God for what His will might be. If you are not led to pray anything specific, look for some Scriptures that you know would be God's will in the situation.
3. Don't stop praying (I mean long-range as opposed to the length of time in one sitting) until you feel God is giving you a sense of release over the situation.
4. Submit to His will, no matter how He answers. God more quickly reveals His will to those whom He knows will obey it.

For Further Reading

Prayer: The Great Adventure, David Jeremiah (Multnomah)
Experiencing God, Henry Blackaby and Claude V. King
(Broadman & Holman)

___14

PRAYER PROMISES

As I LOOKED DOWN ON THIS INFANT, I BEGAN TO FEEL FAINT. THE combination of hospital smells and my own sorrow at seeing this little guy—the son of close friends from my church small group—struggle so, started to overwhelm me. Less than a day old, Aidan would prove to have a profound effect upon my faith—both negatively and positively.

Dave and Dawn had known from tests that their baby would have significant health issues. So they were somewhat prepared when he arrived (early)—minus an ear, with a cleft palate, his liver developed outside his body, and suffering heart and lung problems. Almost immediate surgery had corrected the liver problem, though it had to be later redone when weak muscles gave way and split apart.

Despite his facial disfigurements, Aidan was a beautiful baby. And that's not a parent talking! Maybe he was beautiful because God gave me a strong love for this little guy. Maybe his beauty came from the fact that he was loaded with personality—he became a scrapper. At one point they had to tape gauze mittens on his hands because he would try to pull the breathing tube out of his mouth. Several times he succeeded in at least pulling a connection apart.

He fought through open-heart surgery, which included a ride to a Denver hospital and back. He fought through other procedures that poked and prodded and invaded his tiny body.

Our church rallied behind this family in prayer. We prayed like we had never prayed before. We prayed for a miracle in Aidan's life. We prayed with great faith. We prayed in small groups, even corporately as a congregation on Sunday morning. Because of e-mail and Dave and Dawn's network of friends from both the Chicago and Boston areas, I suspect thousands were praying with us.

I'm not usually given to emotion, but Aidan brought it out in me. When I visited him, prayer was always part of my visit. I would stand quietly near him, or sometimes in the hallway outside the Neonatal Intensive Care Unit, and silently cry out to God. I prayed for him, his doctors and nurses, Dave and Dawn—for improvement, breakthrough, and a miracle.

One Saturday, we received word that Aidan wasn't doing well and might not make it through the next twenty-four hours. We hastily assembled a group of friends, and in our living room about sixteen church members stormed the gates of heaven for Aidan. One member saw angels coming around his crib (an unusual vision for our conservative church). Aidan rallied that night and the crisis was over.

We followed the instructions of James 5:14-15: "Is any one of you sick? He should call the elders of the church to pray over him and anoint him with oil in the name of the Lord. And the prayer offered in faith will make the sick person well; the Lord will raise him up." The unit gave us special permission to break the number-of-visitors rule. Five of us gathered around Aidan, anointed him, laid hands on him, and prayed.

On another occasion (three and a half months into his life) I got a call that he might die any minute. Following his heart surgery and his trip back to Colorado Springs, fluids and an infection were now building up in his body. He was having trouble breathing as both his heart and lungs were beginning to get squeezed by the liquid. Our pastor was away, so as an elder I rushed to the hospital not knowing if I would have to minister to grieving parents—something I had never done before. I was crying all the way, pleading with God to spare Aidan and at the same time asking for words to share with grieving parents and grandparents.

The liquid made Aidan look huge—and in such pain. Clearly he was losing his fight. But as family and friends prayed together in a side room, Aidan relaxed and started rallying again.

All the while I clung to promises in Scripture:

If you remain in me and my words remain in you, ask whatever you wish, and it will be given you. (John 15:7)

Dear friends, if our hearts do not condemn us, we have confidence before God and receive from him anything we ask, because we obey his commands and do what pleases him. (1 John 3:21-22)

This is the confidence we have in approaching God: that if we ask anything according to his will, he hears us. And if we know that he hears us—whatever we ask—we know that we have what we asked of him. (1 John 5:14-15)

[Jesus said,] "Again, I tell you that if two of you on earth agree about anything you ask for, it will be done for you by my Father in heaven." (Matthew 18:19)

We asked, and asked, and asked. We agreed, agreed, and agreed! I started asking God, "Is there a key? Are You trying to teach us something?" I began thinking about an intercession story I had recently read in Dutch Sheets's book *Intercessory Prayer*. It seems a woman asked him to pray for her sister who was comatose in a nursing home. She had been there in that state for a year and a half. There was no hope. Even if she ever woke up, she would be a vegetable. He agreed to go and pray for her—and got hooked. Dutch went once a week for more than a year and prayed by her bedside for at least an hour each time. Then, after more than two years in a coma, the woman awoke, her brain fully restored![1]

One day, my pastor Doug and I were prayerwalking through our church's neighborhood. We talked about Aidan. I shared with him Sheets's story and said that since it was so much on my mind, I wondered if God didn't want us to do some sort of "bedside prayer vigil" of our own on Aidan's behalf. I had thought it out. We could get volunteers to sit by Aidan's crib and pray. We would make sure that once a day, someone was there praying for an hour.

I felt a peace. As the prayer coordinator of our church, I wanted some experiences that would show God's great power when we prayed. I think I even thanked God for the miracle He was going to bring. I went home excited and recharged.

Aidan died the next day.

That was in the summer and fall of 1999 and it still shapes me as an intercessor—especially as I think about God's promises about prayer.

—— WHY THE ILLUSTRATION?

By now you are thinking, *Why did you use a "negative" story in a chapter on prayer promises? Wouldn't an illustration that showed where two people agreed in prayer and God miraculously moved have been better?* Maybe. As a person whose spiritual gift is faith (remember chapter 12), it would have been easy for me to excite you with the words of these promises. Imagine, if two of you agree, God will give you what you want! Think about it, ask whatever you wish and God will give it! I could have told stories that demonstrate this. But the fact remains that not all prayers where two people agree are answered in the way they asked. Not everything we ask for—no matter how "good a Christian" we are—is given to us.

So why put these promises in Scripture if they are not true? Ah, but they are true! It is often our interpretation of them or our understanding of what they mean that gets in the way. We have to remember three things as we learn about prayer promises: (1) Every promise I mentioned—and there are others as well, such as Luke 11:5-13, John 14:12-14, Jeremiah 33:3, and 2 Chronicles 7:14—sits in the middle of a passage of Scripture. We have to look at each verse in light of the rest of the passage to fully understand it. (2) Most promises have conditions attached to them. We have to ask: Are our lives meeting the conditions of the text for us to even be able to claim these promises? (3) These promises have to be understood within the bigger picture of "the theology of answered prayer." For example, is an understanding of God's will in a situation more important than the power of our agreement? In other words, does the condition of 1 John 5:14-15 (praying in God's will) become more important than the situation of Matthew 18:19 (agreement with some other pray-er)?

Let's look at these points more closely. I will cover the first two together because they are closely related.

—— CONTEXT AND CONDITIONS

While I cannot cover every prayer promise mentioned in Scripture, I hope you will gain some principles to use in studying the other promises. To understand the issues of context and conditions, let's look at the promises in John 15, 1 John 5, and Matthew 18.

The first promise, John 15:7, is by far one of the most quoted prayer promises, often used to bolster the faith of people who are praying about a difficult situation: "If you remain in me and my words remain in you, ask whatever you wish, and it will be given you." Is this a promise that any Christian, no matter who she is, no matter how deep her relationship with Christ, can claim? No. We can immediately see the condition: remaining in Christ and having an understanding of His words (the Bible).

This verse sits in the middle of the passage about Christ being the Vine and believers the vine branches (John 15:1-16). The passage mentions bearing fruit as a proof of this remaining, or "abiding," as the King James translates the word. This "fruit" that our lives should display can mean both the fruit of the Spirit (Galatians 5:22-23) and the fruit that grows the kingdom of God (Mark 4:20). In other words, if we are "remaining" in Christ, our lives will reflect a growing Christlikeness and we will somehow impact others (seeing them come to Christ or grow in Christ).

The passage also indicates that as branches, we will receive our sustenance from Christ, the Vine. This seems to hint at the idea that if our lives are truly coming from Him, we will want what He wants and ask for what He would ask for (including things like love for each other, John 15:17).

But does that mean this verse is not true at face value? Will God not grant "things" to us if we are abiding in Him?

My mother's life has been a model of this verse in action. Mom is a lover of God. To me, she is a clear example of what it means to abide in Christ. And more than almost anyone I know, she has received answers to her prayers for specific "things" (not that she asks for things often). In a very real way I believe

God responds to her because she has met the conditions of this passage. Two examples come to mind.

For years, Mom was music director at a Christian summer camp. She always threw her heart and soul into her work, wanting to glorify God with music. One summer she had arranged a musical piece that required a brass choir. The piece was designed to put groups of brass instruments all around the outside of the thousand-plus-seat tabernacle. But Mom needed one more trombone for the piece to work right. She knew another trombone player was on the campground, but he didn't have his trombone. Mom prayed, asking God to supply a trombone. As she was walking back to her quarters, a friend called out a window to her, "How are things going, Doris?" As Mom started explaining the situation, she saw two boys approach from down the street. One of them was carrying a trombone case! "Why do we ever doubt God?" the woman said. The boy let Mom borrow the trombone that evening. Later, as she was relating this story to another friend, Mom said God answered her prayer because, "God must surely love brass music." "No," responded the friend, "God loves Doris Graf."

Another instance of answered prayer occurred when Mom was in college. Since her father had died when she was young and her mother worked in a low-paying job, Mom had to put herself through school. But God provided. One time she was accompanying the choir on piano when the organist reminded her that she should wear something dressy for an upcoming concert. Mom had nothing fancy. After thinking and praying about it, she told the organist that if she found money in her mailbox that morning, she would know that God wanted her to buy a new dress. She did. But after buying the dress, of course she realized black suede shoes would be nice too. Later that day a friend of hers brought a box into her room. "These were sent to me and they don't fit," the friend said. "Can you use them?"

She pulled out a pair of black suede shoes in just my mom's size.

Yes, God will even respond to requests for things, but I do not believe this verse is a "claim all" promise. It must be used in the context of a life that pleases the Lord and relies upon Him for everything.

The second promise, 1 John 5:14-15, also has conditions and a context: "This is the confidence we have in approaching God: that if we ask anything according to his will, he hears us. And if we know that he hears us—whatever we ask—we know that we have what we asked of him." Its condition: We must ask according to His will. The context: It lies in a passage describing the traits of a true believer. John wrote to believers who were being infiltrated by false teachers, explaining to them how to recognize someone who is false and what makes us real followers of Christ. Within that framework he prayed: If you believe in Jesus Christ and ask anything that you know is His will, He will hear and answer.

This promise too is no "catchall" for always getting what we want. We discern God's will and pray for it to come about. For a more complete understanding of prayer and God's will, reread chapter 13. One of the most powerful uses of this promise is to claim and pray for things in our lives that we know to be God's will for us. Chapters 10 and 11 give us help, but here's another illustration. Prayer leader Al Vander Griend relates a time in his life when this passage became a reality:

> To ask for what is according to God's will is to ask for the very things He wants for us. These are the things He knows we need, the things that are truly good for us, the riches of His grace that He wants us to have.
>
> How do we know what is according to His will? We look in the Bible. There God tells us what He wants for us.

When I first understood this principle and wanted to pray in accord with God's will, the Holy Spirit took me to Romans 8:29 and reminded me that God wanted me "to be conformed to the likeness of his Son." Then I did a very simple thing. I said, "God, please conform me to the image of Your Son." That was the first prayer I consciously prayed in accord with God's will. God heard me and began in me the process that answered that prayer. He's still working at it today.[2]

While I don't believe this promise is limited solely to spiritual growth, I do agree with Vander Griend. I think the best way to operate in this promise is to look for things in Scripture that you know God desires for you and to concentrate on praying for them to happen in your life.

The third promise, "If two of you on earth agree about anything you ask for, it will be done for you by my Father in heaven" (Matthew 18:19), clearly has a context. It sits amid a passage that covers conflicts and forgiveness between individuals (verses 15-35). If we take the "context" position that all these verses relate to each other, then our use of the promise is very limited. The prior verses give instructions on how to deal with an individual who sins against you (go to him; if still unresolved, take a witness; finally, take it to the church). So the idea seems to be that if you win back a brother with whom you were at odds, you now operate in agreement, and "anything you ask . . . will be done for you." If we hold the position that this verse fits with the context of what comes before, then the emphasis of the passage isn't prayer, and the promise only "works" in a reconciliation situation.

But there are other context issues to consider as well, specifically two issues. First, did Jesus speak the words of Matthew 18:19 at the same time and place that He spoke the previous verses? We often rely on the subheads in our Bibles to put "related verses" together. But in the original Scriptures, there are no verse divisions, let alone subheads, to guide us. It is very possible that the two sections (verses 15-17 and 18-20) were not spoken at the same time. Second, even if they were spoken at the same time, in our record of Jesus' words He often went from one topic to another very quickly. The Sermon on the Mount (Matthew 5–7) is loaded with multiple topics. So where does that leave us?

Many believers—myself included—do claim this prayer promise in situations other than unity issues. We know from experience that agreement in prayer is very powerful. But like our other prayer promises, there are conditions here. This verse does not simply mean that two or more Christians who pray for the same thing will get what they want. In the case of Aidan, hundreds of believers, many of them "top-level" prayer warriors, were praying for healing and health, for a miracle. No miracle came (at least not the visible miracle we were praying for). Did that mean the promise is untrue? No, other principles were in operation as well. Verse 20 gives us the condition: "For where two or three come together in my name . . . " This idea of coming together in Christ's name holds with it all the implications of praying in Jesus' name. One major implication is praying according to His will. Therefore, we will see the truth of this promise in action only if we are praying in agreement with God's will in that situation. We pray that, and it will be done. Perhaps in Aidan's case, God's will was different from ours. We prayed the obvious solution—heal him. But God had significant kingdom purposes in a short life for Aidan. When we seek to claim this promise, we need to be sure that what we are agreeing on is God's will.

—— THE BIGGER PICTURE

We also need to look at these promises in light of the theology of answered prayer. When it comes to answered prayer, I believe two aspects reign supreme: God's sovereignty and God's will. Throw in the principles of unanswered prayer that we'll cover in the next chapter, and you will be better able to fit these promises into the big picture.

I firmly believe that prayer releases God's will on earth. I also believe that Scripture offers proof that at times God even changes His mind as a result of prayer (that's another book!). But above all, I have a deep respect for God's sovereignty. No matter what I want, no matter what I think I need, no matter if I believe I understand God's will in a situation, I still have to trust God to do what is best. He is in complete control of all things—both good and evil—and I need to trust Him.

Aidan's death—coming on the heels of something I believed God was directing me to do—threw me for a tremendous faith loop. For a time, my ability to believe God for just about anything in prayer waned. But like other situations we cannot explain, I finally had to come back to the truth that God is in control. I can't understand the hows and whys of what He did in Aidan's situation. But I can rest in this truth: He knew best. His purposes were ultimately good.

We also must remember to claim these promises only as they relate to God's will. I would much rather see something happen—even something hard, even something I wasn't praying—knowing it is God's will for me.

Back in the 1970s, my dad applied for a parachurch ministry position that he knew he would really love, one that would make use of his many administrative gifts and in a location where he had spent the happiest days of his life. He and my mom prayed a great deal about the job. He didn't get it. Out of that time my mother in particular started to pray that God would bring something into Dad's life the excitement of which would far surpass the loss of his dream job.

God did. Dad found out about Evangelism Explosion, a soul-winning training program for individuals and churches. He took the training and started using it in his church. While Dad had seen people come to Christ previous to this training, nothing prepared him for the exciting ride this was to bring him for the rest of his ministry. Over the course of the next twenty years, Dad had the opportunity to see hundreds come to Christ, leading many of them to Jesus himself. He saw greater growth in his churches. He trained scores of people in how to share their faith. Those people trained others. Today, my father could very well have had a hand in a thousand or more believers being in the kingdom, all because he and my mom wanted God's will above what they thought was best.

So What?

Does this mean we should not look seriously at prayer promises? By no means! Claim them in situations. They will build your faith and the faith of others. And James 5:17, among other verses, tells us that God honors faith.

But also claim them understanding their conditions. Is what you are asking for God's will? Are you abiding in Christ? Are you on what saints of old called "praying ground," in other words, in a right relationship with God?

Continue to ask God to take you deeper in your dependence upon Jesus as the Vine, so you can reach that level of abiding of which the apostle John wrote. Pray for His will to be done in all situations. Ask Him to give you knowledge of His will, and pray that. And then as He leads, claim a promise He gives you.

For Further Reading

"Claiming Promises in Prayer," Alan Andrews and Jonathan
Graf (*Pray!* Issue 24, May/June 2001)
The Incredible Power of Prayer, David W. Balsiger, Joetter Whims,
and Melody Hunskor (Tyndale)
Developing a Prayer-Care-Share Lifestyle, Alvin J. Vander Griend
et al. (Hope Ministries)
"Keys to the Kingdom," Alvin J. Vander Griend (*Pray!* Issue 7,
July/August 1998)

__ 15

HINDRANCES TO PRAYER

YOU DON'T HAVE TO BE A BELIEVER FOR LONG TO COME UPON A feeling that your prayers are not going anywhere. You try to pray, but the words just seem to hit the ceiling. It seems as if God is not paying any attention. Or you may be praying regularly, but no longer see any answers to your prayers.

There are times in our spiritual growth when God deliberately seems distant from us. Perhaps He is teaching us something about Himself, so He sends us through a "dark valley." These times, however, will be extremely rare—maybe once or twice in a lifetime. More likely, we have run up against one of the hindrances to prayer mentioned in Scripture. When this happens, we can do some simple things to get back on the right track.

I remember one of those times in my life was in the late '80s. After the breakup of my marriage, I had turned to the Lord in a way I had never done before. And it was a wonderful time of spiritual growth. God answered significant, specific prayers almost weekly. I had never experienced anything like it. I was learning to depend upon Him and trust Him for everything. But about six months later, that sense of God's presence and blessing seemed to stop almost overnight. What had happened? I had run smack dab into one of those hindrances!

During this time of rapid growth and blessing, God was continually dealing with me about things in my life. He was refining me, making me more Christlike. During this time He revealed a need to stop using sarcasm as a form of humor. And He gave me victory over it. He was also dealing with me about a chair in my apartment (sounds silly, but read on). But I was not so quick to respond and obey what He wanted me to do.

It was a comfy leather office chair that I had inherited from a former roommate in 1981. Because of some legal problems, my roommate moved out in a hurry and left several pieces of furniture with me. When we had both been students at a Christian liberal arts college, Jeff (not his real name) had been a security guard with access to all the buildings on campus. One night he had stolen this chair from a storage room where a new shipment of furniture had been delivered. I hadn't stolen the chair; it had been stolen well before we even roomed together. I was not responsible for the sin surrounding that chair. But I knew its origins—and God asked me to make it right.

I spent the better part of several months justifying why I didn't need to do that. After a while, the convicting voice of the Holy Spirit left me. But so too did any sense of God's presence when I prayed, as did the regularity of answered prayer.

My prayer life—and overall Christian life—had been affected by this biblical truth: "If I regard iniquity in my heart, the Lord will not hear" (Psalm 66:18, NKJV), or as the New International Version puts it, "If I had cherished sin in my heart, the Lord would not have listened." Scripture teaches that when we keep known sin in our lives, God *does not even hear* our prayers!

Writing about this truth, A. W. Tozer, popular writer and pastor of a half-century ago, said,

When we go to God with a request that He modify the existing situation for us, that is, that He answer prayer, there are two conditions that we must meet: (1) We must pray in the will of God, and (2) we must be on what old-fashioned Christians often call "praying ground"; that is, we must be living lives pleasing to God.

It is futile to beg God to act contrary to His revealed purposes. To pray with confidence, the petitioner must be certain that his request falls within the broad will of God for His people.

The second condition is also vitally important. God has not placed Himself under obligation to honor the requests of worldly, carnal, or disobedient Christians. He hears and answers the prayers only of those who walk in His way.[1]

First John 3:21-22 reminds us: "Dear friends, if our hearts do not condemn us, we have confidence before God and receive from him anything we ask, because we obey his commands and do what pleases him." *If* our hearts do not condemn us, we will receive what we ask. Sin in our lives condemns us. Not that we have lost our salvation, but if we refuse to deal with sin we have lost our access to God!

If your prayers don't seem to be going anywhere, look first at the possibility of sin in your life. As you go to prayer, ask the Holy Spirit if anything stands between you and God. Then listen, and confess what is revealed to you. Don't justify anything away!

In my situation, God first gently began convicting me, putting the thought about the chair into my heart. But it wasn't until I justified it away that He stopped hearing my prayers. A few months later I did deal with the situation. I went to an alumni gathering, where I confessed to the school's president my role in having the chair and gave him a check to pay for it.

The president smiled and asked me if Jeff had been my room-mate. It seemed that God recently had moved Jeff to pay for the chair too! The main benefit, though, was that when I obeyed God and dealt with this sin, His presence and power returned to my prayer life.

Billy Graham was once asked what changed in his life that caused his ministry to explode. He named three things, one of which was that he learned to daily confess his own sins.

Prayer leader Mell Winger tells of a time when he experienced a couple of weeks of unusual spiritual dryness. As he started analyzing the situation he realized that, compared to normal times when devotions seem emotionless, this felt more like his prayers were literally being blocked. He relates that 1 Peter 3:7 popped into his mind: "Husbands, in the same way be considerate as you live with your wives, and treat them with respect as the weaker partner and as heirs with you of the gracious gift of life, so that nothing will hinder your prayers." Remembering a recent incident of being unkind to his wife, he confessed it to the Lord and then to his wife. The dryness left and he once again felt like he was connecting in prayer.[2]

According to Winger, Scripture actually lists fifteen things that hinder prayer:

- Rejecting truth (Proverbs 28:9)
- Pride (2 Chronicles 7:14)
- Hard-heartedness (Zechariah 7:12-13)
- Lack of compassion (Proverbs 21:13)
- Unconfessed sin (Psalm 66:18)
- Wrong motives (James 4:3)
- Unbelief (Matthew 17:20-21)
- Not seriously asking (James 4:2)
- Broken relationships (1 Peter 3:7)
- Sinful lifestyle (Isaiah 59:2)
- Vain repetitions (Matthew 6:7)

- Lack of forgiveness (Matthew 6:14-15)
- Hypocrisy (Luke 18:9-14)
- Double-mindedness (James 1:5-8)
- Idolatry (Ezekiel 14:3)[3]

By now you may be thinking, *Okay, Jon, you've convinced me. A sin-free life is important for power in prayer. But what do I do—I'm human; I sin all the time. Does that mean God never hears my prayers?*

Of course not. Remember our key verse, Psalm 66:18—it says, "If I had cherished [or regarded] sin . . . " The word translated *regard* is key. It implies knowledge of or refusal to give up sin.

It doesn't necessarily mean if in a moment of frustration I'm unkind to a salesclerk that my prayer life is over. But if I have a habit of getting testy with people when I am frustrated and refuse to deal with that before the Lord, I believe God doesn't hear my prayers—until I come to Him in humble repentance.

When some people discuss Psalm 66:18, they are quick to emphasize that a person has to willfully refuse to give up a sin for consequences to kick in. Personally, I don't agree. God's standard is to be perfect as He is perfect. I find it hard to believe that with all the warnings to confess sin, to come with hearts that don't condemn us, God just overlooks our heart's condition when we want to come into His presence.

Psalm 24:3-4 says, "Who may ascend the hill of the LORD? Who may stand in his holy place? He who has clean hands and a pure heart." And James 4:17 tells us, "Anyone, then, who knows the good he ought to do and doesn't do it, sins." So, in other words, if we fail to do something we know we should do, we have sinned.

What's my point?

Too many of us ignore or make light of things in our lives that the Bible calls sin. We live with a temper and call it a character trait. We live with a hidden pornography problem and pass it off as harmless "looking." We live with bitterness and unforgiveness from broken relationships or past hurts and point the finger of blame at someone else. Yet each is sin, and if we harbor it, our prayer life is powerless.

So What?

While I do not want you to get overly paranoid about this issue, I do believe it is extremely important. So how can you protect yourself from "prayer block"?

- Keep a short account with God. Confess sins regularly. That's why so many of the prayer acronyms, like ACTS, include confession as a part of the prayer agenda. It is a necessity.
- Ask the Holy Spirit to search your heart and reveal anything that has come between Him and you. Then confess it and repent of it — turn away.
- Make every effort to live a pure life!

Rest assured that God wants to be in relationship with you. He wants to open up the lines of communication as much as you do. He will be quick to show you what's wrong if you simply ask. Don't let one of these hindrances destroy your prayer life!

For Further Reading

A Time to Pray God's Way, Evelyn Christenson (Harvest House)
Man: The Dwelling Place of God, A. W. Tozer (Christian Publications)
Power Through Prayer, E. M. Bounds (Baker)
Developing the Secret Closet of Prayer, Richard A. Burr (Christian Publications)

—– 16

PERSEVERING PRAYER

WHEN HER OLDER SISTER WAS KICKED OUT OF THE HOUSE BECAUSE of her lifestyle, eleven-year-old Tricia McCary began to cry out to God to bring her back—both to home and to Him. She prayed for more than a decade until her prayers were answered.[1] Sandie, hurt by a wayward husband who left her for a homosexual lifestyle, suddenly became burdened to pray for him. She prayed fervently for years, until at last he returned home. Parents prayed for a son who had forsaken his spiritual upbringing and joined a cult. Over time God led them to claim specific verses to help their unbelief. Eventually their son left the cult.[2] George Mueller, the famous nineteenth-century ministry leader, kept a prayer list of nonChristian friends. Year after year he prayed for them. One by one they began turning their lives over to Jesus. The last one came to Christ at Mueller's funeral.

These stories represent decades of prayer, not a concept that's easy to live with in our fast-paced society. We're so used to microwaves (two minutes and ready to eat), fast-food restaurants (five minutes and we're out the door), credit cards (why save up when we can buy it now), and hundreds of other timesaving conveniences that waiting for anything becomes an almost impossible feat. Yet if we are to grow in prayer, we must learn to wait. We have to learn to keep on praying, even when the answer doesn't seem to come.

It's called persevering prayer. Others use the phrase "praying through." Basically, it means we must continue praying until God answers—even if it takes years. In His plans and purposes, God doesn't always answer prayer right away. But that doesn't mean we should stop. He often has His own timing in situations, or He wants to teach us something along the way. Either way, we wait.

▬▬ JESUS ON PERSEVERING

On several occasions Jesus taught His followers the necessity of being diligent in prayer.

> *"Suppose one of you has a friend, and he goes to him at midnight and says, 'Friend, lend me three loaves of bread, because a friend of mine on a journey has come to me, and I have nothing to set before him.'*
>
> *"Then the one inside answers, 'Don't bother me. The door is already locked, and my children are with me in bed. I can't get up and give you anything.' I tell you, though he will not get up and give him the bread because he is his friend, yet because of the man's boldness he will get up and give him as much as he needs.*
>
> *"So I say to you: Ask and it will be given to you; seek and you will find; knock and the door will be opened to you. For everyone who asks receives; he who seeks finds; and to him who knocks, the door will be opened." (Luke 11:5-10)*

Then Jesus told his disciples a parable to show them that
they should always pray and not give up. He said, "In a
certain town there was a judge who neither feared God nor
cared about men. And there was a widow in that town
who kept coming to him with the plea, 'Grant me justice
against my adversary.'

"For some time he refused. But finally he said to him-
self, 'Even though I don't fear God or care about men, yet
because this widow keeps bothering me, I will see that she
gets justice, so that she won't eventually wear me out with
her coming!'"

And the Lord said, "Listen to what the unjust judge
says. And will not God bring about justice for his chosen
ones, who cry out to him day and night? Will he keep put-
ting them off? I tell you, he will see that they get justice,
and quickly." (Luke 18:1-8)

In the parallel passage recorded in Matthew, Jesus followed
up those verses by commenting, "Which of you, if his son asks
for bread, will give him a stone? Or if he asks for a fish, will give
him a snake? If you then, though you are evil, know how to give
good gifts to your children, how much more will your Father in
heaven give good gifts to those who ask him!" (Matthew 7:9-11).

What do these passages teach us about persevering?
Certainly God cannot be compared to a grumpy neighbor or an
unjust judge. Yet Scripture clearly says that Jesus told the parable
to teach about persevering in prayer. In the first Luke text, the
word *boldness* carries with it the idea of continuing to bug, not
giving up until you have what you need. The King James Version
translates the term *importunity*. Webster's Dictionary defines
importune as "to urge or entreat persistently or repeatedly."

Clearly Jesus is saying if you haven't received an answer
right away, don't give up. Don't pray once and forget it. Keep

asking. He's even giving permission for us to "bug" God. Bible scholars agree that the verb tenses in Luke 11:10 literally mean "ask *and keep on asking,* seek *and keep on seeking,* knock *and keep on knocking."* It is a continuous action.

The apostle Paul also talked about this earnest, prolonged persistence in prayer. He instructed the Colossian believers to "continue earnestly in prayer, being vigilant in it with thanksgiving" (Colossians 4:2, NKJV). You mean not only keep it up, but also be thankful for the wait? Yes, that's right. Paul told the believers in Rome to "join me in my struggle" by praying (Romans 15:30). In another passage, Paul described this perseverance as "wrestling": "[Epaphras] is *always wrestling* in prayer for you, that you may stand firm in all the will of God, mature and fully assured" (Colossians 4:12, emphasis added).

⟶ Isn't Prayer Easy?

By now you may be thinking, *I thought this book was supposed to encourage me. Tell me that prayer is simple, easy.* Sorry. I did say simple; I didn't say easy. There are aspects of prayer in which we need to grow that are not easy (persistence being one of them). They are painful and hard. A struggle—even wrestling.

But why would God make us wait, make us struggle? Here are a number of possible reasons:

The timing isn't right. God is the master at doing things at the perfect time. Often when I look back at situations, I see value in why something happened when it did (always later than I wanted!).

One clear example was the start-up of *Pray!* magazine. As we developed the idea for *Pray!,* our goal was to launch it on the National Day of Prayer in 1996. But as we tried to raise funds in 1995, we ran up against a brick wall! We prayed a lot. Many prayer leaders prayed as well. At virtually every prayer gathering I went to that year, people gathered around me, laid hands on me, and prayed for the funds. Nothing!

The next year came and went. We continued praying. I'm not sure I have ever prayed as much on one single issue in my life. Several times I went to the mountains to spend a good part of the day in prayer. I did a three-day fast. In November 1996 my boss told me that if the funds or a promise of the funds hadn't come in by February 1, 1997, we would walk away from the project. He would give me six months of work while I looked for another job.

The third week of January, a foundation promised the remaining funds. We launched on the 1997 National Day of Prayer. Why did God wait to respond? What possible difference could one year have made? Plenty!

As I look back, I can clearly see three reasons why God waited. First, *I* wasn't ready—spiritually, knowledge-wise, and network-wise. The training ground God put me on in those two years was tremendous. I learned so much about prayer, about prayer ministries, about what God wanted the magazine to be. If we had launched in early 1996, I think we would have failed.

My boss wasn't ready. In late 1995, our associate publisher was promoted to publisher. His replacement was not ready to launch a magazine—a very risky venture with an industry success rate of less than 25 percent. Peter—my new boss—needed time to get on board with the vision and to understand the purpose of *Pray!* before he risked. He also wasn't ready theologically. Our magazine would cross evangelical and charismatic theological boundaries. He needed time to understand and accept that idea.

Our staff wasn't ready. *Pray!* would be the new kid on the block. It would add work to those employees who had responsibilities on all three NavPress magazines. It added work, but no increase in staff or pay. A number of these individuals were not happy with the idea of launching a new magazine. The extra year was needed to either get them on board or shift responsibilities to someone else.

To this day, I praise God that He made us wait, that He didn't answer our pleas on our time schedule. With hindsight, I can clearly understand that His timing was perfect.

God wants to show His love. For those of us who like things to happen quickly, this may sound odd, but sometimes God has us wait because He simply wants to spend time with us. Missionary giant Adoniram Judson held this view:

> God loves importunate prayer so much that He will not give us much blessing without it. And the reason He loves such prayer is that He loves us, and knows that it is a necessary preparation for our receiving the richest blessing He is waiting and longing to bestow.
>
> I never prayed sincerely and earnestly for anything but it came at some time—no matter at how distant a day, somehow, in some shape, probably the last I would have devised, it came.[3]

In my own life this has been true as well. Over and over I have learned that it is those things about which I persevere that are so much sweeter than answers or blessings that come quickly. Why? Because I learn and experience more of God's love as I spend time with Him in prayer.

God needs to change our motives. Sometimes we must wait because our motives and desires are wrong. James said, "When you ask, you do not receive, because you ask with wrong motives, that you may spend what you get on your pleasures" (James 4:3). Perhaps we are asking for something out of selfish motives, or pride is in the way. God needs time to alter that wrong attitude. Or perhaps, He doesn't respond because of sin in our life (see chapter 15).

We don't want it enough. Sometimes God simply wants us to care more about what we are asking for. God told the prophet Jeremiah, "You will seek me and find me when you seek me with all your heart" (29:13). If we come to God with a ho-hum attitude about something or if we quit praying too easily, we will not "find God."

Jesus' parables on this matter focus on determination. Keep asking! How many times do my prayers for a situation or person in need lack that passion? I'm sorry to say many times I pray for things simply to say I've covered them. I told so and so I would pray for a certain need. I should pray for my family, so I do it out of duty. I don't do it with a persevering passion that says, "I'm going to storm heaven until I see God move in this area!"

God wants to teach us something. When we become believers in Jesus Christ, God puts us in school. The course? Christlikeness 101. That's the ultimate work God is doing in our lives: conforming us to the image of His Son. Much of that character building is done through our prayer experience. God wants us to learn dependence, trust, humility, and so on. Perseverance teaches much in this regard.

J. Oswald Sanders once wrote,

> Importunity is one of the instructors in God's training school for Christian culture. It may be that God does not grant the answer to a prayer at once because the petitioner is not yet in a fit state to receive what he or she asks. There is something God desires to do in the believer before He answers prayer. There may be some lack of yieldedness or some failure to master the previous spiritual lesson. So while He does not deny the request, He withholds the answer until, through persevering prayer, the end He has in view is achieved.[4]

So What?

My main point: Don't give up! Just because you don't see an answer right away doesn't mean you should stop praying. I've known people who've prayed years for something—the salvation of a loved one, healing, and so on—before they saw an answer.

God says, "My thoughts are not your thoughts, neither are your ways my ways" (Isaiah 55:8). Sometimes we simply have to trust in His sovereignty and timing. If you persevere in prayer and trust God, you will grow tremendously. God wants that for you. Trust Him!

Jeanne Zornes reminds us,

> God's middle name is "mystery" and His nature is wisdom. Sometimes we may not know the outcome of an unanswered prayer until we set foot in heaven. Then we'll know that it was answered, but in ways we didn't understand.
>
> Martin Luther is credited with saying, "I have held many things in my hands, and lost them all. But whatever I put in God's hands, that I still possess." This is the picture of prevailing prayer. By putting our desires in His hands, we'll possess His blessings.[5]

For Further Reading

Prayer, Ole Hallesby (Augsburg)
The Best of E. M. Bounds, E. M. Bounds (Baker)
With Christ in the School of Prayer, Andrew Murray (Whitaker House)

— 17

EMOTIONS AND PRAYER

I KNEW MY DAUGHTER WAS UPSET. SHE HAD BEEN WOUNDED BY A friend and was trying to deal with the pain. Standing down the hall from her room, I couldn't make out what she was saying. But I heard the emotional pitch—up and down—of her words. Anger and hurt were spewing forth.

No one was in the room with her. Was she talking to herself? Did we need to be concerned? Seek counseling for her? No. Amy was praying.

Amy has learned to take her hurts to God. Not given to the silent way her mother and I pray, Amy often talks to God out loud. And she always expresses her emotion, whether happy, angry, hurt, or depressed. And she'll approach God at any time, anywhere. The shower is a favorite spot. When she is happy, she's not even beneath approaching God with an opening, "Whaaatt's uuupppp!"

I love that about her. God has done something special in her heart that allows her to approach Him in this way. She comes with no masks, and He meets her!

One of the most amazing things about Amy's prayer experiences is how she resolves her prayers. Very regularly, when she goes to God hurt and angry, she comes away accepting and at peace.

Expressing emotion in prayer is a gift! Many believers—myself included—find it very hard to do. Somewhere along our Christian journey, we became more staid in our prayer life, less emotional. But God wants to commune with us, even in our various emotional states and even when our anger is directed toward Him. It doesn't matter; He listens.

Scripture backs up the idea that God wants us to come to Him with all our emotions.

⚊⚊ OLD TESTAMENT EXAMPLES

The writers of the Psalms had no fear of holding back. They let their emotions fly, sometimes even offending the senses of us staid prayers.

In Psalm 71, the psalmist was so angry he called for the death of those who had harmed him.

> *For my enemies speak against me;*
> *those who wait to kill me conspire together.*
> *They say, "God has forsaken him;*
> *pursue him and seize him, for no one will rescue him."*
> *Be not far from me, O God;*
> *come quickly, O my God, to help me.*
> *May my accusers perish in shame;*
> *may those who want to harm me*
> *be covered with scorn and disgrace.*
> *But as for me, I will always have hope;*
> *I will praise you more and more.*
> *My mouth will tell of your righteousness,*
> *of your salvation all day long,*
> *though I know not its measure. (verses 10-15)*

In Psalm 80, the writer directed his anger toward God Himself.

> *Awaken your might;*
> > *come and save us.*
> *Restore us, O God;*
> > *make your face shine upon us,*
> > *that we may be saved.*
> *O LORD God Almighty,*
> > *how long will your anger smolder*
> > *against the prayers of your people?*
> *You have fed them with the bread of tears;*
> > *you have made them drink tears by the bowlful.*
> *You have made us a source of contention to our neighbors,*
> > *and our enemies mock us.*
> *Restore us, O God Almighty;*
> > *make your face shine upon us,*
> > *that we may be saved. . . .*
> *Return to us, O God Almighty!*
> > *Look down from heaven and see! (verses 2-7,14)*

Psalm 140 also shows a man overcome by pain, hurt, and frustration.

> *Do not grant the wicked their desires, O LORD;*
> > *do not let their plans succeed,*
> > *or they will become proud.*
> *Let the heads of those who surround me*
> > *be covered with the trouble their lips have caused.*
> *Let burning coals fall upon them;*
> > *may they be thrown into the fire,*
> > *into miry pits, never to rise. . . .*

I know that the LORD secures justice for the poor
and upholds the cause of the needy.
Surely the righteous will praise your name
and the upright will live before you. (verses 8-10,12-13)

Other Old Testament characters expressed their emotions in prayer as well. When Scripture describes Elijah's prayers, it says he "was a man just like us" (James 5:17). At one point after a tremendous victory, Elijah was overcome by self-pity because the queen sought to take his life. Scripture tells us that "Elijah was afraid and ran for his life. . . . He himself went a day's journey into the desert. He came to a broom tree, sat down under it and prayed that he might die. 'I have had enough, LORD,' he said. 'Take my life; I am no better than my ancestors'" (1 Kings 19:3-4). Read the rest of the story. God sent angels and then passed by Himself as He ministered to Elijah's emotional need.

Jeremiah was known as the weeping prophet. At one point when Jeremiah's prophecy was not well received, he was beaten and thrown in prison. After his release, Jeremiah railed at God:

O LORD, you deceived me, and I was deceived;
you overpowered me and prevailed.
I am ridiculed all day long;
everyone mocks me.
Whenever I speak, I cry out
proclaiming violence and destruction.
So the word of the LORD has brought me
insult and reproach all day long.
But if I say, "I will not mention him
or speak any more in his name,"
his word is in my heart like a fire,
a fire shut up in my bones. . . .

O LORD Almighty, you who examine the righteous
    and probe the heart and mind,
let me see your vengeance upon them,
    for to you I have committed my cause.
Sing to the LORD!
    Give praise to the LORD!
He rescues the life of the needy
    from the hands of the wicked.
Cursed be the day I was born! (Jeremiah 20:7-9,12-14)

One interesting note: these Old Testament examples resolved their hurt and anger by focusing on God's nature and past faithfulness. Elijah, the psalmists, and Jeremiah—just like Amy—were met by God in their pain and came away at peace. Perhaps that points us to an important truth about expressing our emotion to God. When we are honest with Him, He does something in our souls to ease the pain.

⸺ NEW TESTAMENT EXAMPLES

What was Jesus' prayer life like when it came to expressing His emotions? The writer of Hebrews described it by saying, "During the days of Jesus' life on earth, he offered up prayers and petitions with loud cries and tears to the one who could save him from death, and he was heard because of his reverent submission" (5:7).

Such intense emotion is certainly apparent in Jesus' prayer in the Garden of Gethsemane on the night of His arrest.

Jesus went with his disciples to a place called Gethsemane,
and he said to them, "Sit here while I go over there and
pray." He took Peter and the two sons of Zebedee along
with him, and he began to be sorrowful and troubled. Then

*he said to them, "My soul is overwhelmed with sorrow to
the point of death. Stay here and keep watch with me."*

*Going a little farther, he fell with his face to the
ground and prayed, "My Father, if it is possible, may this
cup be taken from me. Yet not as I will, but as you will."*

*Then he returned to his disciples and found them
sleeping. "Could you men not keep watch with me for one
hour?" he asked Peter. "Watch and pray so that you will
not fall into temptation. The spirit is willing, but the body
is weak."*

*He went away a second time and prayed, "My Father,
if it is not possible for this cup to be taken away unless I
drink it, may your will be done." (Matthew 26:36-42)*

Luke's version of this experience tells us Jesus was in such
anguish that he sweat drops of blood, and an angel had to be
sent to strengthen and encourage Him.

Like the earlier Old Testament examples, Jesus too
reached resolution. He was not necessarily at peace about
what lay ahead, but His emotional release brought the
strength and courage to accept the Father's will. Writing on
this issue, Dr. Lloyd Terrell, said, "There are times when we
believers have trials and tribulations, and our fervent prayers
seem not to reach God. But if we can manage to hold out our
deepest feelings to God in prayer, His grace and love will walk
us through that garden of suffering, just like He did with
Jesus."[1]

Because I seldom express raw emotion, my lack of it in
prayer bothered me. If you are like that as well, take comfort.
Terrell points out that "how emotional we are when we pray is
not the important matter at all. What we learn from the prayers
of Jesus is that praying must be real and honest."[2]

— — BEING HONEST

Honesty opens doors to real comfort and peace. Honesty in most human relationships usually builds them instead of tearing them down. And as with earthly relationships, when we are open with God, it will draw us closer. But just as many of us pull away or withdraw from potential conflict in earthly relationships rather than express how we feel and work through it, so too in our relationship with God. "When we get mad at God for something we think God could have helped us avoid," says Timothy Jones, "we are tempted to walk away or pull back. We are not sure our churning emotions belong in the presence of God. We become reserved, and often not too motivated to pray."[3] Jones goes on to say,

> I believe our emotions—all of them—belong in our prayers. . . . Our prayers represent not just what we say but who we are, with all our complex longings and feelings. To be close to someone, even when that someone is God, will inevitably run us through a gamut of emotions. To think prayer should be a monochrome patter is to rob it of its power. To read the Psalms or other devotional outpourings of prayers classical and contemporary is to witness a dazzling emotional tapestry. A wide and sometimes wild range of feelings accompanies a walk with God.[4]

SO WHAT?

If you learn nothing more from this chapter, learn this: Emotions and prayer mix! It is okay to be emotional with God. We do not need to hold back because of some sense of protocol. God wants us to be open and honest. When we are, we can truly be touched and healed.

When I experience pain and frustration in life, I tend to quickly conclude that God is sovereign and this is a part of His will. I even take pride in how fast I accept my "fate." But because I find it hard to express my emotions, I accept that truth on the surface even though it's unresolved in my heart. I still am angry over the situation. I've accepted it, but I still suffer pain and turmoil. I wish I were like Amy. When she expresses her pain, she truly gets relief. In fact, I am amazed at how quickly she forgives those who have angered or disappointed her.

As you grow in prayer, grow here as well. Ask God to help you express yourself and not to hold back. That is my prayer for myself as well.

Don't be afraid where it takes you. God can handle the emotion.

For Further Reading

A Love Affair with God, C. Welton Gaddy (Broadman & Holman)
The Art of Prayer, Timothy Jones (Ballantine Books)
The Intercessory Prayer of Jesus, Warren Wiersbe (Baker)

——18

FASTING AND PRAYER

W E NEEDED ANSWERS. THE THOUGHT HAD COME TO MY WIFE TO buy a house big enough so my parents, who were retiring after forty-plus years of ministry, could live with us. Two of their three sons lived in Colorado Springs; it would seem a logical place for them to settle down.

We had only been in our small house a little over two years. How would we possibly swing the expense of a larger house, let alone have the funds to remodel it to add an apartment? The thought wouldn't leave us, but it seemed absurd. Was this of God? Or was it simply our own thinking, brought on by a strong sense of wanting to provide for my parents?

As we prayed about it, a sense of peace wouldn't fully come. We continued moving forward, looking at houses and builders. Now we had reached a decision point. Put up or shut up.

It was then that God led us to spend a day fasting and praying over this issue. And clarity came. We signed a contract on a new house and put our house on the market. It sold—for our asking price—to the first couple that looked at it.

Now, more than three years later, it has proven to be a wonderful decision.

—— WHAT'S FASTING, ANYWAY?

By now you may be thinking, *What is fasting and should I make it part of my prayer life?*

In its simplest form, fasting means denying yourself food for a period of time. Some people who fast drink only water during that specified period; others drink any liquid. A "Daniel Fast," based on the passage in Daniel 1 where Daniel and his friends did not eat the rich food offered in the palace, limits the participant to vegetables and water.

Other people fast from certain things for a period of time: television, sports, sexual relations (1 Corinthians 7:3-5). For the purposes of this chapter, we are talking about food fasts. While I believe other fasts are legitimate, fasts from food and sexual relations are the only type mentioned in Scripture.

Why fast? What does fasting accomplish that won't happen if I simply pray? To answer those questions, let's look at the purposes for fasting. Put simply, "Fasting helps us to subject our bodies to our spirits," says author Cindy Hyle Bezek. "When we fail to discipline our bodies, sin often results."[1] Fasting helps to subordinate our fleshly desires to our spiritual ones. It shows humility and dependence, and demonstrates to God how serious we are about a matter.

Bill Bright, founder and former president of Campus Crusade for Christ, has been used mightily of God to bring fasting back to the evangelical church. In his book *The Coming Revival*, he lists seven reasons to fast:

1. Fasting is a primary means of restoration. By humbling us, fasting releases the Holy Spirit to do His revival work within us. This takes us deeper into the Christlife and gives us a greater awareness of God's reality and presence in our lives.

2. Fasting reduces the power of self so that the Holy Spirit can do a more intense work within us.
3. Fasting helps to purify us spiritually.
4. Fasting increases our spiritual reception by quieting our minds and emotions.
5. Fasting brings a yieldedness, even a holy brokenness, resulting in an inner calm and self-control.
6. Fasting renews spiritual vision.
7. Fasting inspires determination to follow God's revealed plan for your life.[2]

—— SCRIPTURE AND FASTING

I've already referred to Daniel, but how prevalent is fasting in the Bible? Of the sixty-six books in the Old and New Testaments, thirty of them mention fasting. It seems to have been practiced for a variety of reasons.

Jehoshaphat. Armies were massing to attack Judah. King Jehoshaphat knew his nation was in trouble. What did he do? "Alarmed, Jehoshaphat resolved to inquire of the LORD, and he proclaimed a fast for all Judah" (2 Chronicles 20:3). God honored the people's demonstration of dependence with this promise: "The battle is not yours, but God's. . . . You will not have to fight this battle. Take up your positions; stand firm and see the deliverance the LORD will give you" (verses 15,17). Out of this fast came the unusual idea to place singers at the front of the army of Judah and have them simply sing praise to God as they went. Miraculously, the attacking armies simply turned on each other. Jehoshaphat's army just watched the battle!

Commenting on this passage, Ronnie Floyd wrote, "[Jehoshaphat] understood the spiritual practices of fasting and praying. Jehoshaphat knew that to fast before God was the best way to show his complete helplessness and humility before God. He learned something you and I must never forget: He renounced the natural to invoke the supernatural."[3] In this situation of utter helplessness, a nation humbled itself and God did the rest. Fasting can be a good alternative when we come to the end of our rope in a situation. Another example of this kind of fasting is the story of Esther (see Esther 2–4).

Ezra. As the Babylonian captivity was ending, a band of Jews led by Ezra the priest was allowed to return to Jerusalem. Though it would be a dangerous journey through hostile deserts filled with bandits and wild animals, Ezra and his band had King Artaxerxes' blessing to return, along with money from his treasury and a letter telling cities along the way to give this group whatever provisions they needed. There is some indication that the king even offered armed escorts to protect this traveling party. So what was the problem? Why would Ezra feel the need to fast and pray—despite such a promise of support?

"I assembled them at the canal that flows toward Ahava, and we camped there three days, . . ." he wrote.

> *There, by the Ahava Canal, I proclaimed a fast, so that we might humble ourselves before our God and ask him for a safe journey for us and our children, with all our possessions. I was ashamed to ask the king for soldiers and horsemen to protect us from enemies on the road, because we had told the king, "The gracious hand of our God is on everyone who looks to him, but his great anger is against all who forsake him." So we fasted and petitioned our God about this, and he answered our prayer. (Ezra 8:15,21-23)*

Apparently, Ezra wanted to show a secular king the power of God. Even though he could have had man's easy answer to the dangerous situation—soldiers to protect them—Ezra refused. He wanted God to prove Himself mighty. There is no question—both in Scripture and in personal experience—that fasting releases God's power in unusual ways.

I started making fasting a part of my prayer life when *Pray!* was just in its development stage. As we waited for funding, and as I waited for a new boss to "get on board" with a desire to launch the magazine, I stayed very calm and confident—on the outside. I was sure God had brought me to NavPress for something other than my *Discipleship Journal* job years prior. But on the inside I was in a minor turmoil. I had a family to provide for. I would lose my job if *Pray!* didn't happen. Months were passing with no finances coming in, no sign that God was going to act.

It was during this year-long period that I fasted a number of times. Sometimes I would take my Bible and go into the mountains surrounding Glen Eyrie (The Navigators' retreat center in the Rockies). There I would worship, pray, seek God's face, and listen. While no revelations ever came during those days, they did keep me somewhat calm and relaxed, and they renewed my sense to trust God, whatever He was going to do.

It was also during this time—as the deadline to curtail the project approached—that God led me to do something I had never done before. I went on a three-day fast. Again, no revelation came, but shortly thereafter the rest of the needed funds were received and *Pray!* was launched.

Jesus. Jesus Himself fasted in the wilderness at the start of His earthly ministry. Scripture reveals that "after fasting forty days and forty nights, he was hungry" (Matthew 4:2). That's an understatement! Not only was He seeking His Father's direction and strength, but He also was preparing for the test to come—the temptation of Satan. We too should add fasting to our prayers when we are about to embark on a new ministry, a new chapter in our life, something significant that has permanent ramifications.

Jesus also talked about fasting. In the Sermon on the Mount He gave these instructions: "When you fast, do not look somber as the hypocrites do, for they disfigure their faces to show men they are fasting. . . . But when you fast, put oil on your head and wash your face, so that it will not be obvious to men that you are fasting, but only to your Father, who is unseen" (Matthew 6:16-18). From this passage we learn two things. First, fasting is to be done in secret. It is not something we should advertise. If we are serious about it, only God needs to know. I do not believe that means it is always wrong to let anyone know we are fasting. But the precedent of secrecy protects us from pride and false motives. Second, notice that Jesus said, "when you fast," not "if you fast," an indication that fasting should be a regular part of our prayer life.

On another occasion, John the Baptist's disciples came to Jesus and asked, "'How is it that we and the Pharisees fast, but your disciples do not fast?' Jesus answered, 'How can the guests of the bridegroom mourn while he is with them? The time will come when the bridegroom will be taken from them; then they will fast'" (Matthew 9:14-15). This statement is also a charge to us to fast. Jesus (the Bridegroom) is no longer physically with us (the church/believers). Therefore, we need to make fasting part of our prayer discipline.

So What?

If you want to grow in your prayer life, should you fast? Yes! Unless there is a significant medical reason why you cannot, take steps to begin fasting. Start small. If you have never fasted before, during a lunch hour get a drink and your Bible, and instead of eating, read your Bible and pray. You do not need a more specific reason to fast than that you want to humble yourself before God and seek Him.

What happens when you get hungry? Just plow on

174

through. Ignore the pangs and determine to pray through them. It will get easier the more you do it, and the more you get used to your body's sensations. But bear in mind that when you fast, you are engaged in spiritual warfare! Satan hates to see believers deny their flesh. He will do everything he can to stop you. Don't give in!

As you consider taking on a longer fast, another spiritual principle comes into play. In Isaiah 58, an excellent chapter about fasting, God asks, "Is this the kind of fast I have chosen?" (verse 5). That phrase, "I have chosen," appears again in verse 6. The principle: For fasting to be truly powerful, you must be directed by God to do it.

In his classic book on fasting, *God's Chosen Fast*, Arthur Wallis writes,

> On our part, there must be the recognition of the rightness and need of fasting, the willingness for the self-discipline involved, and the exercise of heart before God; but in the final analysis the initiative is His. When we fast, how long we fast, the nature of the fast, and the spiritual objectives we have before us are all God's choice, to which the obedient disciple gladly responds.[1]

Like prayer, fasting originates with God. I would rarely fast longer than a meal unless I felt strongly led by God to do so. As you think about a longer fast, listen for God's prodding and His voice regarding the agenda for this special time with Him. Now, lest you think you need to hear a loud voice or receive a knock on the head, I assure you that it will usually come more subtly than that. As you are praying about something, the thought, *I should fast over this*, might come to you. Obey that thought. Or perhaps one Sunday your pastor says, "We need to really pray about this situation. I hope some would be willing to fast as well." You get a simple prick in your spirit to honor that request. That is enough. At those rare times when you may feel led to fast for a longer period (three, seven, twenty-one, and forty days are the most popular time lengths), I would anticipate receiving a much stronger burden than a simple nudge. Twice in my life I fasted for a longer period. Both times I felt a strong burden to do so.

Let's assume you feel led to fast longer than a meal. The next step is to fast for an entire day. The easiest format is to start after supper one day and wait twenty-four hours before eating again. Remember to take liquids. Another format is to start one morning and go till the next. This is a little harder because you will go to bed hungry.

Okay, you may be thinking, *I'm going to fast for a day. What about prayer? How much should I pray?* My simple solution is to try to pray during times when I would have eaten. If possible, I also try to pray throughout the day as hunger pangs become strong. This gives me a sense of overcoming my flesh. I do not beat myself up over how much time I pray when fasting. As God puts it on my mind, I pray.

My mother, whom you read about in earlier chapters, commented, "I have never had a fasting experience but what unusual, explicit answers have come." Now hypoglycemic and no longer able to do a food fast, she misses it. She recently told me how profitable it has been in her spiritual life, recalling one time when in a burst of passion, she told God, "Lord, it would be wonderful to share how much I love You with other people." Before the day was out she received a call requesting that she speak at a statewide women's conference.

Why not start your own adventure with fasting?

For Further Reading

The Transforming Power of Fasting and Prayer, Bill Bright (New Life Publications)

The Power of Prayer and Fasting, Ronnie Floyd (Broadman & Holman)

"Fasting: Partake of God's Holy Feast," Cindy Hyle, Bill Bright, and Arthur Wallis (*Pray!* Issue 3, November/December 1997). Go to *www.praymag.com*, click on "Search the Archives," and type in "fasting" on the search engine.

God's Chosen Fast, Arthur Wallis (Christian Literature Crusade)

-–19

THE PRAYER OF FAITH —
THE KEY TO IT ALL

STEVE WAS A NEW BELIEVER WHO ATTENDED OUR SINGLES MINISTRY at Immanuel Alliance Church in Mechanicsburg, Pennsylvania. Steve's wife had recently left him, and due to some medical issues and medication he was taking that impaired his senses, he had lost his job as a truck driver. He was clearly in need of prayer.

During prayer time at our Thursday night Bible study, I began to pray aloud for Steve. My prayer started out normally. I simply lifted up Steve's needs. To be honest, I wasn't particularly close to Steve, so my prayers were not born out of deep love or concern but rather out of the thought, *Uh oh, someone better pray for Steve's need.* Sometime during the prayer, passion took over. Because it was more than twelve years ago, I don't remember any specifics of what I prayed. But because it was such a profound and rare experience for me, I can remember clearly what I was thinking and feeling throughout the prayer.

I recall that my spirit got so caught up in praying for Steve that I didn't even know *what* I was praying. I remember a strange but pleasant sensation within my body and feeling my mind so riveted on the prayer it was like I was staring at the situation and couldn't pull away. I remember others pitching in comments of agreement as I prayed. About halfway through my prayer, an unusual thought entered my head: *I'm not praying; the Holy Spirit is praying within me.*

After the prayer, Steve immediately came over and hugged me—for longer than I was comfortable. He had sensed something unusual too.

Because I left that group a few months later, I don't know what ultimately happened to Steve's marriage; I do know his job situation resolved soon after that night.

What made that prayer so powerful? So unusual? Did I do something special? No! While I can't fully know for sure what did happen, I believe that my prayer for Steve brought together so many of the elements of effective prayer.

First, I was pure before the Lord. This was during the time when I was working on the A. W. Tozer project and was immersed in *The Pursuit of God.* I was hungry for God; I was delighting in God; I was experiencing God in deeper ways than I had ever experienced before.

Second, while I didn't have a strong relationship with Steve, I could relate to his pain. My divorce had been finalized only months before. As I prayed, my own pain reemerged. That led to a release of my emotions—usually bottled up when I prayed in public.

Third, everything I prayed was fully in line with God's will. God did not desire Steve's marriage to break up. God fought for the brokenhearted, the poor and downcast, the one who was being treated unfairly. To pray for restoration of Steve's marriage and job was fully in harmony with God's will.

Fourth, my thought of the Holy Spirit praying through me was in a sense very accurate. I have no doubt that I was praying what I "ought to pray for" (Romans 8:26). I was in some way caught up in the "groans that words cannot express" that the Spirit prays.

Finally, it was a prayer of faith—the key to it all. I believed perhaps more than I had believed anything in my life that God was going to do something special in Steve's life. Steve was a new believer, and the Lord was going to prove Himself to Steve. Steve needed a miracle, and God was going to provide one. There was absolutely no doubt in my mind.

—— PRAYING IN FAITH

James tells us that God answers "the prayer offered in faith" (5:15). Earlier in his book, James wrote, "If any of you lacks wisdom, he should ask God, who gives generously to all without finding fault, and it will be given to him. But when he asks, *he must believe and not doubt*" (1:5-6, emphasis added).

When Jesus' disciples asked Him why they couldn't drive out a particular demon possessing a little boy, He replied, "Because you have so little faith. I tell you the truth, if you have faith as small as a mustard seed, you can say to this mountain, 'Move from here to there' and it will move. Nothing will be impossible for you" (Matthew 17:20).

Above all else, it is the prayer of faith that God honors. All of the principles in this book are pointless without this one undergirding them all.

Why do we need to develop a relationship with God through prayer? The more we know Him, the more we trust Him, the more faith will grow within us.

How are we involved in seeing God's will released on earth if not through prayers of faith? We believe that our prayers can and do make a difference in this world, so we keep praying.

How do we keep going amid fears that our prayers are weak, feeble, and ineffective? Faith. We believe God's Word when it says both the Holy Spirit and Jesus are interceding when we don't know what to pray. Faith tells us our prayers are amounting to something, even when we doubt.

What allows us to communicate with God anywhere? Faith. Faith to believe that God is with us always.

It takes faith to believe God hears and will respond. It takes faith to believe that we are victorious over the evil one and that we have access to all authority!

Every aspect of prayer involves faith!

So What?

God wants to commune with you. Believe it! God wants to use you in awesome ways to further His kingdom. Pray for it! He wants to make a prayer warrior out of you. Accept it by faith.

If you are still struggling, still unsure of this prayer thing, then I invite you to pray a simple prayer. It is the same prayer a scared, frustrated father cried out to Jesus after being told, "Everything is possible for him who believes":

"I do believe; help me overcome my unbelief!"
(Mark 9:23-24)

Enjoy the ride!

For Further Reading

Fresh Faith, Jim Cymbala (Zondervan)
The Prayer of Jabez, Dr. Bruce Wilkinson (Multnomah)

⎯⎯ NOTES

⎯⎯ CHAPTER 1: WHAT IS PRAYER?

1. C. Welton Gaddy, *A Love Affair with God* (Nashville: Broadman & Holman Publishers, 1995), p. 19.
2. Alvin J. Vander Griend et al., *Developing a Prayer-Care-Share Lifestyle* (Grand Rapids, MI: HOPE Ministries, 1999), p. 12.
3. A. B. Simpson, *When the Comforter Came* (Camp Hill, PA: Christian Publications, 1911, 1991), p. 87.
4. Dutch Sheets, "Does God Really Need Our Prayer?" *Pray!* 11, March/April 1999, p. 19.
5. Sheets, p.19.
6. E. M. Bounds, *The Best of E. M. Bounds* (Grand Rapids, MI: Baker, 1981), p. 76.
7. A. W. Tozer, *Who Put Jesus on the Cross?* (Camp Hill, PA: Christian Publications, 1975), p. 103.
8. A. B. Simpson, *The Christ in the Bible Commentary, Vol. 3* (Camp Hill, PA: Christian Publications, 1993), p. 498.
9. A. B. Simpson, *The Christ in the Bible Commentary, Vol. 5* (Camp Hill, PA: Christian Publications, 1994), p. 459.

⎯⎯ CHAPTER 3: WHERE DO I PRAY?

1. Sandie Higley, "So What's the Big Deal about a Prayer Closet?" *Pray!* 7, July/August 1998, pp. 26-27.

2. Higley, p. 27.
3. David Trembley, "Body Language: Praying with Your Whole Self," *Pray!* 12, May/June 1999, pp. 26-29.
4. Trembley, pp. 27-29.

—— CHAPTER 4: TO WHOM SHOULD I PRAY?

1. Alvin J. Vander Griend et al., *Developing a Prayer-Care-Share Lifestyle* (Grand Rapids, MI: HOPE Ministries, 1999), pp. 30-31.
2. Samuel Chadwick, *The Path of Prayer* (London: Hodder & Stoughton, 1936), p. 52.

—— CHAPTER 5: THE PRAYER OF PETITION

1. "An Interview with Mentor, Lee Brase," *Pray!* 17, March/April 2000, p. 17.
2. Dr. Bruce Wilkinson, *The Prayer of Jabez* (Sisters, OR: Multnomah, 2000), p. 23.
3. Wilkinson, p. 24.
4. Todd Gaddis, "Dare to Pray the Jabez Way," *Pray!* 25, November/December 1999, p. 13.
5. Alvin J. Vander Griend et al., *Developing a Prayer-Care-Share Lifestyle* (Grand Rapids, MI: HOPE Ministries, 1999), p. 40.

—— CHAPTER 6: THE PRAYER OF INTERCESSION

1. Steve Hawthorne, "Intercession in the King's Court: Presenting a Case Before the Throne of God," *Pray!* 11, March/April 1999, pp. 20-23.
2. Joy Dawson, *Intercession, Thrilling and Fulfilling* (Seattle: YWAM Publishing, 1997), pp. 30-31.

—•— CHAPTER 7: HEARING GOD'S VOICE

1. Timothy Jones, "Why Am I Doing All the Talking?" *Pray!* 13, July/August 1999 p. 10. Article adapted from *21 Days to a Better Quiet Time with God* (Zondervan) © 1998 by Timothy Jones. This article can be found at *www.praymag.com*.
2. Marilyn Heavilin, "Is That You, Lord?" *Pray!* 13, July/August 1999, p. 19.
3. Heavilin, p. 19.
4. Heavilin, p. 20.
5. Rebecca Livermore, "Excuse Me, Lord?" *Pray!* 4, January/February 1998, p. 31.

—•— CHAPTER 8: PRAYERS OF ADORATION AND THANKSGIVING

1. Joan Esherick, "Consumed with the Person of God," *Pray!* 15, January/February 2000, p. 27.
2. Timothy Jones, *The Art of Prayer* (New York: Ballantine Books, 1997), p. 89.
3. Lee Brase, "Prayer Tunes Our Hearts to God," *Pray!* 11, March/April 1999, p. 37.
4. Jack Hayford, *The Heart of Praise* (Ventura, CA: Regal, 1992), pp. 26-27.
5. Ole Hallesby, *Prayer* (Minneapolis, MN: Augsburg Fortress, 1931), p. 141.
6. Henry Blackaby and Claude V. King, *Experiencing God* (Nashville: Broadman & Holman, 1994), pp. 175-183.

—•— CHAPTER 9: SPIRITUAL WARFARE PRAYER

1. Tom White, "Families Under Attack," *Pray!* 5, March/April 1998, p. 17.

2. Mell Winger, "Praise as a Weapon," *Pray!* 5, March/April 1998, p. 25.
3. White, p. 18.

—— CHAPTER 10: PRAYING SCRIPTURE

1. Jane McClain, "His Word Will Not Return Empty," *Pray!* 13, July/August 1999, p. 26.
2. Bob Hostetler, "31 Biblical Virtues to Pray for Your Kids," *Pray!* 4, January/February 1998, p. 34. This article is available at *www.praymag.com*. Click on "Xtras." You can also get copies on card stock.
3. McClain, p. 27.

—— CHAPTER 12: FINDING YOUR PRAYER STYLE

1. Alice Smith, "Praying Together: Annoying or Anointed," *Pray!* 6, May/June 1998, p. 33. Article adapted from *Beyond the Veil: Entering into Intimacy with God through Prayer* by Alice Smith (Regal, 1998).
2. Adapted from Smith, pp. 33-34.
3. Mark Phillips, "Take Your Prayer Closet on the Road," *Pray!* 22, January/February 2001, p. 14.

—— CHAPTER 13: PRAYER AND GOD'S WILL

1. Sandie Higley, "As It Is in Heaven," *Pray!* 11, March/April 1999, p. 25.
2. Dick Eastman, "George Mueller's Six-Step Plan for Seeking God's Will," *Pray!* 13, July/August 1999, p.17.
3. J. Oswald Sanders, *Prayer Power Unlimited* (Grand Rapids, MI: Discovery House Publishers, 1977), p. 52.

—— CHAPTER 14: PRAYER PROMISES

1. Dutch Sheets, *Intercessory Prayer* (Ventura, CA: Regal, 1996),
   pp. 15-18.
2. Alvin J. Vander Griend et al., *Developing a Prayer-Care-Share
   Lifestyle* (Grand Rapids, MI: Hope Ministries, 1999), p. 42.

—— CHAPTER 15: HINDRANCES TO PRAYER

1. A. W. Tozer, "Does God Always Answer Prayer?" *Pray!* 4,
   January/February 1998, p. 37. This article was excerpted
   from *Man: The Dwelling Place of God* (Christian Publications).
2. Mell Winger, "What Hinders Prayer?" *Pray!* 10,
   January/February 1999, p. 29.
3. Winger, p. 30.

—— CHAPTER 16: PERSEVERING PRAYER

1. Tricia McCary Rhodes, "A Sister's Prayer & God's Timing,"
   Pray! 3, November/December 1997, pp. 34-36.
2. William Hanford, "Help My Unbelief!" *Pray!* 16,
   January/February 2000, pp. 30-31.
3. Quoted in E. M. Bounds, *Purpose in Prayer* (New York: Revell,
   1910), p. 54.
4. J. Oswald Sanders, *Prayer Power Unlimited* (Grand Rapids,
   MI: Discovery House Publishers, 1997), p. 85.
5. Jeanne Zornes, "Learning to Wait," *Pray!* 2, September/
   October 1997, p. 31.

—— CHAPTER 17: EMOTIONS AND PRAYER

1. Dr. Lloyd Preston Terrell, "The Emotional Prayers of Jesus,"
   Pray! 14, September/October 1999, pp. 19-20.

2. Terrell, p. 20.

3. Timothy Jones, *The Art of Prayer* (New York: Ballantine Books, 1997), p. 122.

4. Jones, pp. 122-123.

—•— CHAPTER 18: FASTING AND PRAYER

1. Cindy Hyle Bezek, "Has the Fast-Food Generation Missed Out?" *Pray!* 3, November/December 1997, p. 17.

2. Bill Bright, "Why Fast?" *Pray!* 3, November/December 1997, p. 29. Adapted from *The Coming Revival: America's Call to Fast, Pray, and "Seek God's Face"* © 1995 Bill Bright.

3. Ronnie Floyd, *The Power of Prayer and Fasting* (Nashville: Broadman & Holman Publishers, 1997), p. 12.

4. Arthur Wallis, "What's in It for Me?" *Pray!* 3, November/December 1997, p. 24. Adapted from *God's Chosen Fast* by Arthur Wallis (Fort Washington, PA: Christian Literature Crusade, 1968).

ABOUT THE AUTHOR

JONATHAN GRAF (B.A. ENGLISH LITERATURE, NYACK COLLEGE; M.Ed. English Education, State University of New York at Buffalo) taught high school English for seven years before starting his publishing career. In 1989 he became the classics editor at Christian Publications, Inc., and a year later was promoted to editorial director. In 1994 he joined NavPress as managing editor of *Discipleship Journal*. Shortly afterward, his idea for *Pray!* was born, and the magazine's first issue launched in 1997.

Jon speaks frequently at churches across the United States, conducting both prayer weekends and prayer seminars. He and his wife, JoLyn, are parents of a teenage daughter, Amy.

IGNITE YOUR PRAYER LIFE!

Pray! Magazine

This bimonthly magazine will revolutionize your thinking about prayer. Includes thought-provoking articles from leaders of the prayer movement, excerpts from classic books on prayer, and effective biblical strategies.
(NavPress)

When God Whispers

This collection of insightful Scripture-based meditations will remind you of the extraordinary love God reveals to us—even in the midst of ordinary days.
(Carole Mayhall)

Becoming a Man of Prayer

Based on Jesus' instructions, this book will help men achieve a deeper prayer life—starting with five minutes each day.
(Bob Beltz)

Becoming a Woman of Prayer

God designed women to seek Him in all they do. This Bible study will encourage you to become a woman whose life is characterized by constant conversation with God.
(Cynthia Heald)

Get your copies today at your local bookstore, visit our website at www.navpress.com, or call (800) 366-7788 and ask for offer #BPA or a FREE catalog of NavPress products.

NAVPRESS
BRINGING TRUTH TO LIFE
www.navpress.com